ROCKHOPPER COPPER

Life and police work on the world's
most remote inhabited island
TRISTAN DA CUNHA

Conrad J. Glass MBE

Edited by Chris Bates

© Conrad J. Glass 2010

All rights reserved, no part of this publication may be reproduced, stored in a retrieval system, or transmitted, in any form or by any means electronic, mechanical, photocopying, recording or otherwise, without permission from Conrad J. Glass or the publishers. The copyright of photographers whose work has been used is reserved and its inclusion here does not imply any claim on copyright or permission by others to reproduce such work.

A catalogue record for this book is available from the British Library.

All maps within this publication are reproduced by permission of the Government of Tristan da Cunha and may not be reproduced by others without their permission. Images of postage stamps are by permission of the Tristan da Cunha Post Office and are their copyright and may not be reproduced under any circumstances.

First published 2005
Second Edition 2011

Published by Polperro Heritage Press
Clifton-upon-Teme
Worcestershire WR6 6EN
United Kingdom

ISBN 978-0955364877

Printed by 4edge Limited
Hockley, Essex
United Kingdom

CONTENTS

Editor's Notes to the Second Edition 5
Foreword 7
Acknowledgments 9
A Brief History of Tristan da Cunha 13
The 1961 Eruption: Through the Eyes of my Family 18
The 1961 Eruption: The Outside World and Home Again ... 27
All in a Day's Work 32
A Saturday at The Patches 36
Conservation Patrol and Policing the Penguins 41
A Day on the Mountain Herding Sheep 57
Search & Rescue Reports 63
Rescue Attempt on Gough Island 72
Tourism and Immigration 79
Visiting Cruise Ships 86
Crewing a Longboat to Nightingale 91
The *Canton*'s Last Voyage 102
Legends of Tristan 111
The Hurricane of 2001 127
Stamps, Coins and Handicrafts 135
Personal Glimpses 138
Appendix: Visiting Tristan da Cunha 157
Glossary 161

Editor's Notes to the the Second Edition

When Conrad Glass published the first edition of *Rockhopper Copper* in 2005 it was an instant success: it soon became apparent as passengers on cruise liners, visitors, residents and people around world bought the book (and patently enjoyed it), that another edition was needed.

That it has taken so long is as Conrad recounts in this updated edition, as much the result of the pace of change on Tristan da Cunha as anything else and also in the intervening time, Conrad served three years as Chief Islander.

Now at last there has been time to bring the work up to date and to include new information, in the hope of satisfying the continuing demand for Conrad's book. I hope this new edition will answer questions about Tristan from those intrigued by this, the most remote inhabited island on our planet and introduce it to those just becoming aware of it.

Life is never quite the same after an encounter with Tristan da Cunha: my interest dates back to childhood (even before the eruption of 1961) when I can recall looking at a photograph taken on the island, which appeared in the *Daily Telegraph*. That interest developed through a fascination with its stamps and with remote places generally. Work at the BBC and the Royal Norwegian Embassy in London occasionally involved Tristan and kindled friendships which flourish today. They led to work on Conrad's first edition and thus to an invitation to visit in 2006. Two years later, I became the Tristan Government's Representative in the UK though I should stress that what appears in this book does not in any way reflect the opinion of that (or any other) Government.

My admiration for the islanders and their way of life continues to grow and I would like to record my thanks to them, to Conrad and his family in particular, for their many kindnesses, generosity and friendship. In giving thanks for help with editing this edition, I would like to thank my wife Julie for her extraordinary patience; my son Rob for his wise counsel; to publisher Jerry Johns of the Polperro Heritage Press for his kindly guidance and practical help and to Michael Swales and Richard Grundy of the Tristan da Cunha Association, for support and guidance. Involvement with the project and with Tristan has enriched my life and enabled me to visit many places of which I could once only dream: in the process, it has introduced me to many extraordinary people.

I hope Conrad's book enables you to share the lives of the people of Tristan da Cunha and similarly, to be enriched by their experiences, philosophies and way of life.

CHRIS BATES
Selly Park, Birmingham
November 2010

Foreword

We may live in a shrinking world, due to increasing ease and lower cost of travel, yet relatively few people have ever visited the world's most isolated inhabited island - Tristan da Cunha. Of those who have, a number have written about the island and its people, mostly from relatively short acquaintance. Now, for the first time, the reader can learn what it is really like to live there from a direct descendant of one of the founders.

This book reveals how the isolation and the ever-present forces of nature have moulded the psyche of Tristan islanders. Through communal effort and teamwork, they not only survive but thrive; they use natural resources for the common good, with a concern for the weak and elderly to whom they also show respect. An important part is played by communication within the community and home has priority, as does their heritage, of which they are justly proud. Yet these are ordinary people, albeit living in an extraordinary place, whose lifestyle is not out of touch with the modern world. They do, however, face the elements, which, in isolation, would be unbearable to many living in a more pampered way. These people show respect for the environment and acknowledge a creative force beyond themselves, which gives them an envied dignity.

The publication of this book (the first edition was published shortly before the islanders celebrated the quincentenary in 2006 of the discovery of Tristan da Cunha), is timely and thoroughly endorsed.

Michael Swales
Co-founder, President and Chairman of the Tristan da Cunha Association.

I dedicate this book to my wife and my son,
who are the motivation for my life.

Acknowledgements

When I first decided to write this book, I did not envisage the amount of work it would take to complete it. Without the help of the following people, my task would have been more difficult. To them, I offer my heartfelt thanks and appreciation. That it sold out completely, enabling me to prepare this updated and re-edited second edition, makes it possible to also thank those who helped with it and so enabled me to achieve an ambition. To all, I offer my heartfelt thanks and appreciation.

To my wife, Sharon, for typing most of the original manuscript, and Marlene Swain for helping her; to my son Leon for his help and advice on computer and IT matters; to Chris Bates for his advice, input and for editing both editions and to his wife Julie, for her endless patience and support while he did so and for their hospitality in Birmingham; to Richard Grundy, James Glass, Gerry Repetto and David Mackenzie for supplying photographs – a special thank you to Brian Rogers, for the photos and use of his facilities; to Michael Swales, co-founder, president and chairman of the Tristan da Cunha Association for his foreword and his help and unwavering support for the project (and for all things to do with Tristan); to Jerry Johns of the Polperro Heritage Press for arranging the first edition for publication and for publishing this second edition; to the late Allan Crawford OBE for supplying maps; to Sir Martin Holdgate CB and Andy and Lorraine Repetto for help and support and to Lars Repetto for help with checking facts, dates and names; to my family past and present who gave me the insight and scope to write this book; to Christine Stone OBE, my teacher and friend, who gave me the inspiration to fulfil a dream and my thanks to the people of Tristan da Cunha who made this dream possible.

To all who have helped make this book possible but who are not named individually for reasons of space or otherwise – thank you: I am deeply grateful for your contribution.

Events in this book are based on my personal experience and hearsay ('oral history' I ought to call it) from other Tristanians. However, in some chapters I had to interweave personal experiences with hearsay from the past and present, to make the story readable.

To the people of Tristan da Cunha: be steadfast to your livelihood. For in it, you have a unique God-given lifestyle, of unprecedented freedom over your destiny, that many people envy but may never have.

Conrad J. Glass MBE

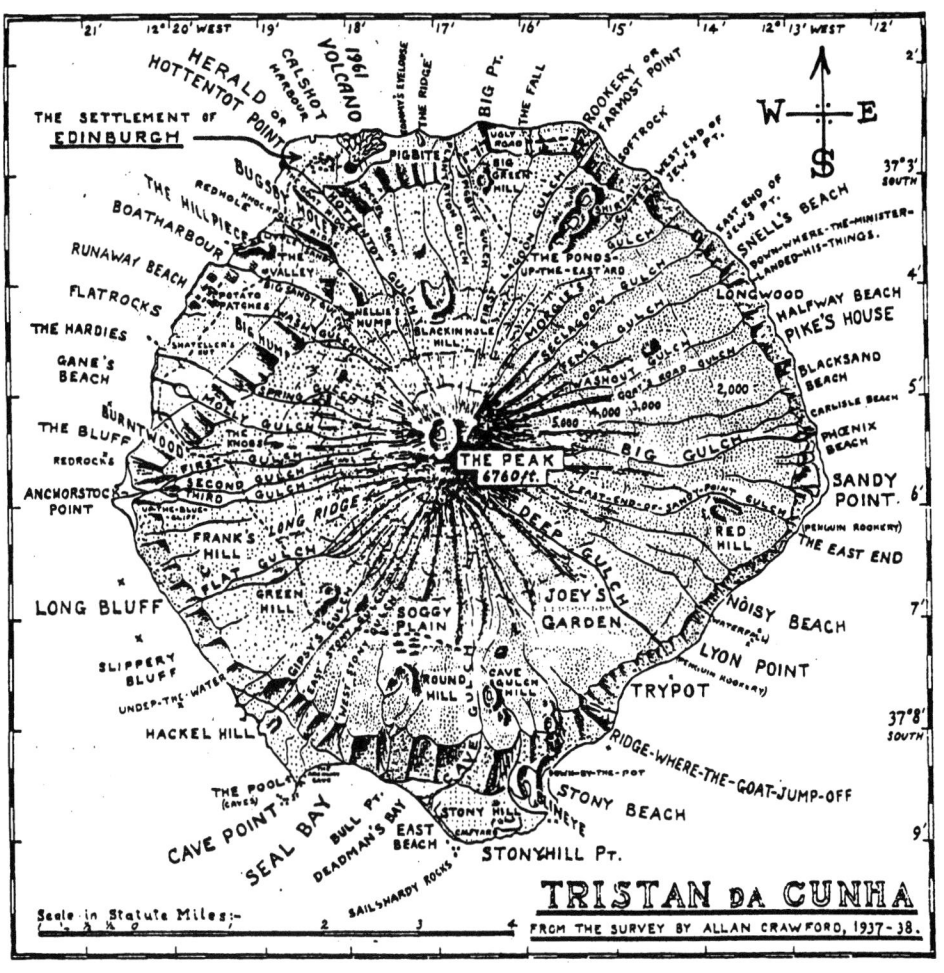

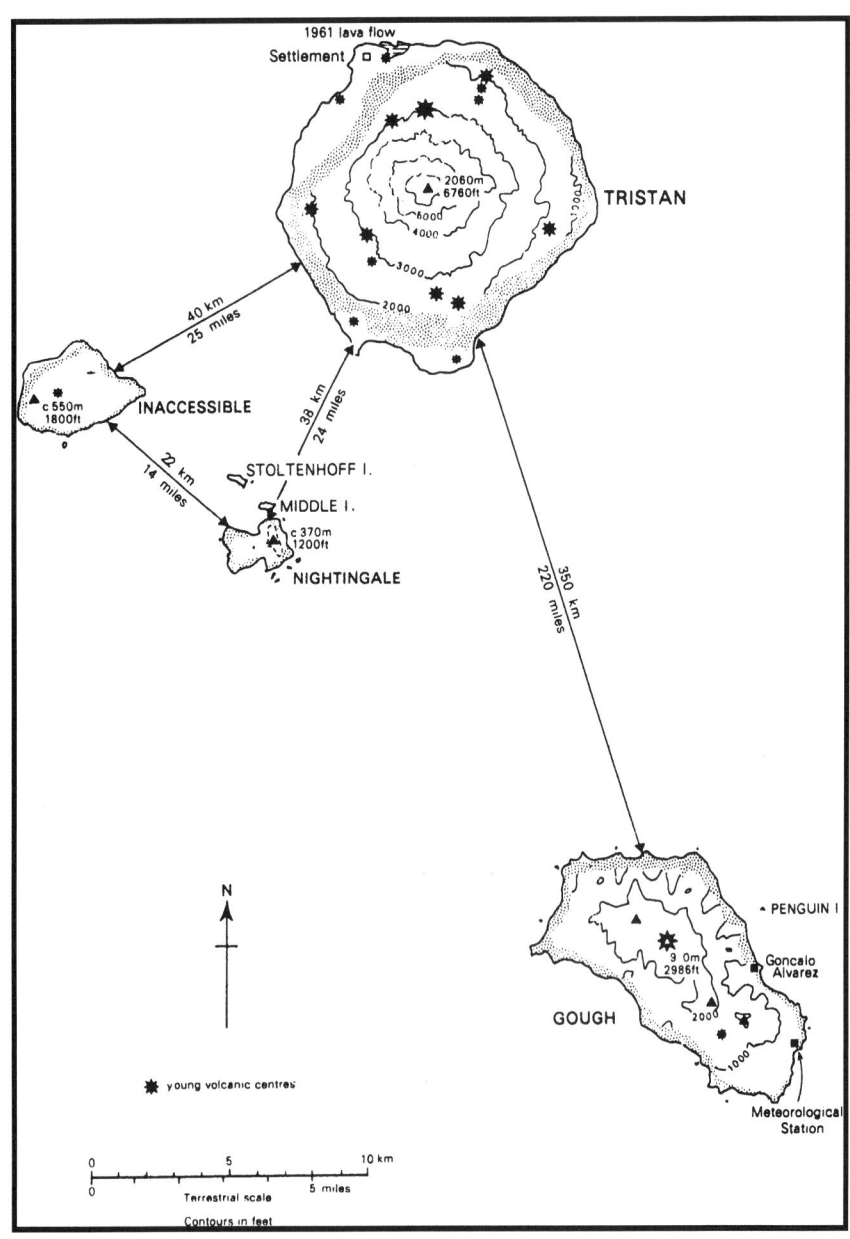

A BRIEF HISTORY OF TRISTAN DA CUNHA

The most remote inhabited island on our planet is Tristan da Cunha.

It's a speck on the map: a very small island in the middle of the South Atlantic Ocean, at 37°6′44″S 12°16′56″W; about 37 square miles, the largest of a group of islands. Inaccessible Island lies (from Anchorstock Point) 18 miles to the west and Nightingale Island 20 miles to the south west. Nightingale is the oldest of the three, and Tristan is the youngest. Gough Island, another of the Tristan group, is located 220 miles to the south of Tristan.

Tristan da Cunha is an active strato-volcano formed above a magma hot-spot some 250 miles east of the Mid-Atlantic Ridge. The volcano first erupted three million years ago from the 11,483 feet deep ocean floor. Successive eruptions have built a cone of 18,044 feet with the summit, Queen Mary's Peak, 6,758 feet above sea level, overlooking a heart-shaped crater lake. On a map, they appear to be part of a chain of islands including St Helena, Ascension, The Azores and Iceland, but the popular supposition that they're part of the Mid-Atlantic Ridge is incorrect. The Hawaiian Islands are similar 'hot-spot volcanoes' in which magma comes from deep within the Earth's mantle, not from gaps between the tectonic plates. The Tristan volcano has many parasitic cones on its flanks, each representing a separate eruption of the main volcano. Around 1750, Stony Hill erupted, producing an extensive black lava field on the southern part of the island.

Cape Town in South Africa is the nearest major port: 1,743 miles away, or six days sailing by ship. St Helena is the nearest inhabited island: 1,510 miles to the north. To Rio de Janeiro, it's 2,083 miles; to Port Stanley in the Falkland Islands, 2,424 miles; to London, 6,140 miles – and there is no airport. The nearest is in Cape Town. There is a timetabled bus service on the island (the most remote scheduled bus service in the world) linking the village or 'The Settlement' of Edinburgh-of-the-Seven-Seas, with The Patches, complete with a bus shelter and bus stops. There has never been a railway on Tristan.

Tristan was first discovered in 1506 by the Portuguese explorer Tristao da Cunha, while en route around the Cape of Good Hope, bound for India. There is no record to say that he landed, but he gave his name to the largest of the three islands before sailing on.

Ships of many European nations visited Tristan over the next century, the greatest number recorded were from Dutch ports. We know the *Buninvis*, bound from Amsterdam to the East Indies in 1601, anchored off Tristan and landed crew on the island.

The first British ship to visit was in May 1610, *The Globe*, an East Indiaman from London. The ships bound for India used Tristan to check their navigation. The first recorded landing by the Dutch was from the *Heemstede* in mid February 1643 (though as noted, men from the *Buninvis* are known to have been on Tristan briefly 42 years before). From 1650 through until the early 1800's, ships continued to visit Tristan, and for several years from 1810, Tristan was used as a base by pirates and buccaneers of American and French vessels, roaming the seas between St Helena and the Cape of Good Hope, lying in wait to raid British merchant ships from the East India Company.

The first people to settle on Tristan were three expatriates, Jonathan Lambert, Andrew Millet, (both American) and Thomas Currie (Irish Italian, also known as Tomasso Corri). Lambert was their leader and they renamed Tristan 'The Island of Refreshment' and invited passing ships to trade with them.

They landed on Tristan on 27th December 1810 and set about clearing land to grow vegetables, rearing chickens, ducks and pigs, with which to barter and trade with passing ships. There is a legend to say that they had an iron chest of treasure with them that formed the proceeds from their wild affrays on the Spanish Main.

The British Government sent a garrison to Tristan just after Napoleon was captured at Waterloo and exiled to St Helena, to prevent Tristan being used as a base by the French to rescue Napoleon. There were also worries about the Americans using the island to attack British shipping. This garrison arrived on 14th August 1816. They established a base called Fort Malcolm and one of its cannons can be seen today outside the Island Museum. When they landed they found only Currie, with a young Spaniard named Bastiano Comilla. Currie told the garrison that Lambert and Millet and another sailor, Williams, had been drowned when their boat overturned whilst out fishing. However, before he died, he hinted, when drunk, of revenge and triumph. He boasted of his treasure of pearls, of diamonds and gold coins, which he produced to pay at the garrison canteen.

The trio were known to have quarrelled but before Currie could reveal the secret of the source of his gold coins, he died and never revealed his secret to the soldiers. No one has ever found his treasure, even to the present day, no matter how much they searched. Legend has it that it was buried somewhere between the two waterfalls. If this is so, then it could be lost forever, buried under tons of lava as a result of Tristan's most recent volcanic eruption.

One of the soldiers was my great-great-grandfather of seven generations, Corporal William Glass, a Scotsman who, when the garrison left, asked for permission to stay behind with his wife (who, as Maria Leenders, he had married before she was 16 in The Cape) and two children, accompanied by two stonemasons, John Nankiel and Samuel Burnell, both Englishmen. He eventually became the island's first governor, and forefather of the present day community.

Over the years, many sailors from passing and wrecked ships have added their mark to the community. Five women from St Helena arrived to become wives of these pioneers. Some sailors married into the community and stayed for a couple of decades, then emigrated to Cape Town, and New Bedford (Massachusetts) in the United States.

There are only seven surnames making up the population of Tristan: Glass (Scotland), Swain (England), Rogers and Hagan (Irish American), Green (Holland), Repetto and Lavarello (Italy). The surnames Riley, Beetham, Taylor, Cotton, Peterson, Pert and Johnson were once represented on the island and so while the names may have gone, their blood still runs in the families that are living on Tristan today.

Over the generations, the islanders have faced many incursions into their way of life beginning from 1937-38, with the arrival of a Norwegian Expedition, which carried out a sociological, environmental and biological survey. It was led by Dr. Erling Christophersen who persuaded a young Englishman, Allan Crawford to join. He produced the first island map, recording unique local place names, such as 'Down Where The Minister Lost His Things', 'Ridge Where The Goat Jump Off' and 'Deadman's Bay'. (Later he became instrumental in helping the island's economic and social development, promoting the development of the fish processing and export industry and the introduction of Tristan's now-famous postage stamps – the early samples were denominated in potatoes!)

On 9th October 1942 during the Second World War, the Royal Navy built a radar wireless station on Tristan and a hospital. This brought about improvements to the lifestyle of Tristanians. For the first time, they had a doctor to care for them. It was also the first time they had worked for a daily wage, helping the Navy to construct their accommodation.

1948 brought about the biggest change in the lifestyle of the island, with the arrival of the MS *Pequena* on a fishing expedition. A private firm, from the South African Government, with the help of the British Colonial Office, organised this venture. The fish they found were endemic to the Tristan archipelago, variously known to the islanders as crawfish, crayfish or Tristan rock lobster – *Jasus tristani*: usually spoken of now as 'crayfish'. They found them in abundance in the waters around Tristan, Nightingale, Inaccessible and Gough. (The fish found off Tristan is sometimes referred to also as 'spiny lobster' but that creature lives in the Mediterranean and the Caribbean and is exported from the Bahamas – it does not live in Tristan waters).

The prospects for the island had never looked so good. A canning factory was built at Big Beach staffed by an expatriate manager. The company also employed an expatriate Agricultural Officer who started a small shop. The men were employed as fishermen to fish from Tristan and on the fishing vessels. The women were also employed on fishing days, processing the crayfish. It was the first time they earned a regular wage. Money started to play an important role in the islanders' lives, as important as their potato patches and their livestock.

By 1950, all the houses in the village had running water. A new sanitary system was laid with outside flush toilets. The British Government had sent a resident administrator, a doctor, a nursing sister, a schoolteacher and a padre (Anglican clergyman): all from the UK. All the children between the ages of five and 15 had to attend school.

A new Community Centre was built, and an Island Council was elected. The fishing ships brought stores, clothes, shoes, soft drinks, milk, sugar, flour, tea, candles, biscuits, paraffin for oil lamps and many other groceries. People ordered stores and were able to maintain their houses to a higher standard. Nails, paint, and wood were brought for houses; canvas for the longboats and a lucky few even had radios and record players.

In all the islanders had never known life to look so rosy. That was, until the eruption of the volcano in 1961...

THE 1961 ERUPTION OF THE VOLCANO: THROUGH THE EYES OF MY FAMILY

Friday 11th August 1961 was a typical day of life on Tristan, with the wind south-west. The gong had been rung and it was a fishing day. The island fishermen were off early in small rowing dinghies to fish for crayfish. The weather was mild, although partly overcast, the sun shone through the breaks in the cloud, shining a greenish grey on the waves. A few families were at The Patches planting the first crop of potatoes for the season. At 9 o' clock, the children went to school as usual. Several men were away fishing on the fishing ships (MFV *Francis Repetto*, and MFV *Tristania 1*); a few were at Stony Beach checking on their cattle.

With the children in school, the women were busy washing before going to the factory at Big Beach to process the fish when the boats arrived back. During this time the crayfish were cooked and packed into tins to sell abroad. This was the only employment for islanders during this era.

It was as peaceful and as tranquil a scene that one could have viewed. The quiet village of stone thatched cottage roofs with smoke spiralling lazily from the chimneys as the islanders cooked their lunch: chickens, cows, and sheep grazed amongst the houses.

Suddenly the peace was shattered as the earth shook, causing small landslides and rocks to crash down the sides of the mountain towards the rear of the village. Inside the houses, walls shook and the crockery and cutlery rattled on the shelves. People ran outside to see what was happening. At the school, several of the young children screamed in terror and held onto their elder brothers and sisters, while the teachers tried to calm them, wondering themselves what was happening. After a few moments, all was quiet. The people three and a half miles away working at The Patches, and the people at Stony Beach, carried on with their tasks, unaware of what was happening back at the village.

People began to gather outside their houses in small groups, talking to each other, and asking the same question. What had caused the village and houses to so suddenly shake, so that rocks crashed down the mountain? The older people reflected and shook their heads in bewilderment; they had not heard or experienced anything like this in the history of Tristan.

The resident Administrator from the UK, Peter Wheeler and the rest of the expatriates conversed: what had happened? Mr Wheeler sent men to the school, the factory at Big Beach and throughout the village to see if there was anyone injured, or property damaged. He sensed in the back of his mind that something sinister was afoot.

Word came back to him that a small landslide had covered some 44 gallon drums of oil near the factory and that some boulders had crashed into the rear wall of the factory, but no one had been injured. Don Binnedell, the factory manager at the time, sent Joe Repetto out with the motor boat to call the fishing boats earlier, informing them of what had taken place.

People who returned from The Patches were amazed when they were told of the events. The village settled down into an uneasy peace: people carrying out their routine chores, the children still attended school, waiting for the earth to start shaking again

That night, after their evening meal, the families sat around their open fires, the interior of the rooms dimly lit by candle or oil lamps. The topic of discussion was the earth suddenly shaking earlier that morning. Word had already spread throughout the village that the people at The Patches had not heard or felt anything. Realising that what they had taken as rumours from a few people in the days before, saying that they had experienced items shaking on shelves on Monday 6th August, had now become facts.

Martha Rogers (known as Auntie Martha), was in one of the groups, and had told some friends that she had experienced cups shaking on the shelf in her kitchen. She was a lady with considerable influence on Tristan and anything she said was not to be taken lightly, so this led to a feeling of concern among many island families.

At this time in its history, the Tristan community had contact with the rest of the world only through the wireless station that kept contact with Cape Town (marine) Radio. Peter Wheeler sent a message to London explaining the facts, seeking advice. The answer came back that there was nothing to be alarmed about, 'it was probably just the earth settling, given that Tristan is a volcanic island', but he was instructed to keep monitoring the situation and keep London informed.

As the days and weeks passed, the 'tremors', as they were called, occurred often on a daily basis, sometimes a couple of times within 24 hours. They became almost part of the lifestyle, but for the fact the quakes were starting to become more violent in their ferocity.

Peter Wheeler told the islanders what London had said. He sent a few teams of men to camp on the mountain to the east of the village, and above the village and at Burntwood. They were to stay up on the mountain for a few days recording the strength of the quakes. The Anglican priest, Father Jewell, went with the men to keep a record of the quakes. They were measured on a scale of one to five: 'one' being only noticeable by items shaking; 'three' the ground shaking; 'five' the whole village shaking, causing rocks and landslides on the sides of the mountain.

The islanders were growing more concerned as August passed into September. The island men fishing on the MFV *Francis Repetto* and MFV *Tristania 1* came back to Tristan to see the results of the tremors for themselves. The ships' captains, who were in daily radio contact with Tristan Radio, had informed them.

My father was fishing on the MFV *Tristania 1* at Nightingale and Inaccessible Islands. At home was my mother, with me being eight months old; my sister four and a half years old; my grandmother, Rose Rogers (who was crippled and could not walk unaided after a stroke years earlier) and my uncle, Gus Rogers. Next door was my mother's sister Aunt Winnie, her husband Nelson Green and nine-year-old son, Jack.

My parents at this stage of the 'tremors' had two travel bags packed with clothes, food, drinks and other items ready to take with them at a moment's notice. Like many people on Tristan, they believed that something worse was about to come. Twice during very heavy quakes at night, when rocks were heard crashing down the mountain causing landslides, my father and Uncle Nelson had both families, with Gran in her wheelchair, at the bottom of the garden. Our houses were built at the rear of the village, near the foot of the mountain, but as it turned out, the quake stopped. All was quiet and they returned to their homes.

The teams of men that were up the mountain monitoring the quakes returned after a few days to report that they had not heard or felt anything. The area of the activity seemed to be concentrated in the village. This was rather disturbing news. Peter Wheeler sent this information back to London, and received an answer to "keep a close eye on things" and he established daily radio contact.

August passed into September. Life on Tristan carried on, with people going about their daily tasks. During the last week of September the tremors increased in ferocity, now at the rate of three to four each day. People found it difficult to shut their doors; the doorposts seemed out of alignment, caused by the shaking of the ground. On Sunday 6th September, the congregation for evensong in St. Mary's Church felt an earthquake: Peter Wheeler describing later how 'the walls heaved, the floors trembled, and for a sickening second, the roof threatened to cave in'. There was a landslide behind the canning factory.

At the first week in October, cracks started to appear in the ground, some closed up again in the east part of the village near the reservoir built at the foot of the mountain. A few days later, some four inch water pipes were pushed out of the ground and bent. Peter Wheeler informed London, and contingency plans were made to evacuate the island if needed. Peter Wheeler also sent men to measure the cracks in the ground. They were growing bigger. During the second week in October cracks started to appear among the houses in the east of the village.

After another earthquake on Sunday 8th October, again during the evening service when there was a massive fall of rock behind the village, Peter Wheeler ordered all families living in the east of the community, to move in with the families whose houses were on the west. During this period a mound appeared in the earth; rising on the sloping terrain of the plateau in the shape of a bubble cone, just 100 metres east of the reservoir, at the top east side of the village. This mound started to grow up to the height of ten feet or more. On top, was a rather large boulder, that had previously fallen down from the cliff above. Fresh soil and small stones tumbled down its sides.

A few hundred yards away, Peter Wheeler and a group of island men watched in horror and awe at these strange phenomena. What unseen force was putting pressure on the earth to create such a mound? As they looked on, a large crack suddenly appeared on the ground close to the mound. Several sheep were grazing nearby. As the crack opened up underneath, the sheep fell into it. Minutes later, the crack closed up again, sealing the sheep's fate forever. This was the moment for action.

Peter Wheeler turned to the group of men and said: "I think it's time to call a meeting of all heads of the families. We will meet in the Prince Philip Hall" [which is the village hall]. The group turned and headed for it. Willie Repetto, the Chief Islander [head councillor] hit the village gong that is used to announce fishing days, deliveries of mail and emergencies.

The word had been spread through the village that a meeting was going to be called. As the gong was rung, men in groups of twos and threes made their way to the Prince Phillip Hall in the centre of the village. There, Mr Wheeler told the men that according to events, he was expecting the mound that was pushing up, to be a new volcano, about to erupt. It would be the safest if the whole community moved out to The Patches for the night. Two tents would be erected at Below The Hill for the sick and people who did not have any huts. The elders and sick people would be taken to The Patches on the tractor, the only vehicle on the island at that time. He also had radioed the Royal Navy for help. HMS *Leopard* had been dispatched from Simons Town (South Africa) to come to their aid.

Around three o' clock on that eventful afternoon, the men left the hall to break the news to their families. Armed with warm clothes, blankets, and food, which was hastily gathered, the entire community trudged the three and a half miles down to The Patches amid light showers of rain from the south west. Many were getting rather wet on the way. My family shared the tents at Below The Hill with Mr Wheeler and many others, because of my grandmother's handicap and my mother and father had to tend to her. My Aunt Agnes took care of me, while my Granny, Liza Glass, took care of my sister during the evacuation. The parents of my wife, Sharon, who were then engaged, later to be married in England, spent the night at Bills Hill in two huts, with their families.

Wet, cold and weary, the islanders settled down to wait the dawn with mixed feelings. The two fishing ships [MFV *Tristania 1* and the MFV *Francis Repetto*] were standing offshore, their crews watching the cone of earth through binoculars, keeping radio contact with Mr Wheeler and Cape Town. There were plans made to evacuate the community aboard the two fishing ships and take them to Nightingale. All would depend on the weather and what happened to the cone of earth. Sharon's grandfather, Cyril Rogers, recalled while at The Patches, he went to collect water from the stream near the bank at Second Watron, only to find that it was hot. He was sharing a hut with my uncle, Sidney Glass, Thomas Glass and their families. A few young island men, Ches and Basil Lavarello, Adam and Soggy Swain, did not sleep that night but spent the time walking around the huts.

No one really slept that night, being wet and uncomfortable, worrying what was going to happen to them. My uncle, Nelson Green, said while most of the people in the tent tried to sleep, he and Peter Wheeler sat having a cup of coffee. Mr Wheeler confided in him, telling him that there was a Dutch liner headed this way to take the islanders off if needed. At three thirty, one of the island men called Mr Wheeler, saying that the ships were trying to contact him on the radio. Rubbing the sleep from his eyes Mr Wheeler grabbed the radio as Captain Scott's voice came through: "It's finally happened, Peter," he said. "The bubble has burst, throwing up cinders of burning rock and belching clouds of smoke."

All the men were sent for again. The news of the eruption was received with a gloomy silence by most. A few exclaimed they heard something that sounded like an empty drum being hit. At first light, it was planned that some men would go back to the village and launch some longboats. They would take the people off from Boat Harbour Bay near the Hill Piece. They would be put onto the ship and taken to Nightingale. Those who were too old or too sick to walk across the beach to Boat Harbour, would be lowered down the cliff face at Big Sandy Gulch; also, most of the islander's belongings were lowered.

The men dispersed to inform their families of the plan. As most of the younger island men set off back to launch some boats, the rest of the community headed for Boat Harbour. When the men entered the village, they saw the looming cone of a new volcano, where the mound had been, smoking and throwing red glowing cinders down its side. Not stopping to stare, the men continued to Big Beach, to get their boats. As they crossed the main stream at the east of the village called Big Watron, they saw that the water had turned to the colour of milk and was quite hot to touch. The *Canton* and *British Flag* were the first two longboats launched, with Lawrence Lavarello and Thomas Glass at the helm.

On reaching Boat Harbour, they found most of the community watching from the beach and cliffs. On approaching the beach, they found a heavy swell running. While *Canton* stood off, Lawrence took the *British Flag* into the edge of the breaking surf. Timing the moment right, Lawrence ordered his crew to row for the beach, catching a breaking wave. *British Flag* surfed onto the beach with Lawrence standing up straight and solid at the steering oar. When the boats hit the beach, many willing hands grabbed and pulled her up, away from the surf, quickly turning the boat around for launching. It was loaded with women and children. Sharon's grandmother, Helen Rogers, with most of her family, were amongst them. Her mother, Catherine Glass, had carried her brother Colin Rogers all the way across the beach, only to find that she then had to carry him all the way home to the village, to be put into the boats there.

As the volcano did not seem that dangerous, and because of the huge swell at Boat Harbour, it was not ideal for many of the community to access. It was decided that it would be quicker for the rest of the people to return home, where they would be taken off at Little Beach to the waiting MFV *Tristania 1* and MFV *Francis Repetto*. As the *British Flag* was launched into the surf, the rest of the people turned and walked wearily back to the village. The elderly were put on to the tractor. Cyril was on his way back from Boat Harbour, having put Helen and most of his children in the boat. When he met Sidney at Old Pieces, he was helping to put people on to the tractor. The news reached them that Annie Swain [my great-great-grandmother] who was in her eighties, had been on her way to Boat Harbour, when she was told that she had to turn back. Her daughter, Agnes Swain, assisted her. (She also died later in England). On reaching Runaway Beach, she could get no further.

Without hesitation, Sidney and Cyril caught a donkey and set off to help. Between them, they got her up from the beach, on to the donkey and back to the village.

My Granny Lisa had told me that on her way back to the village, she stopped at her house to collect some clothes. As she got to Big Watron, she was so tired that she dragged the bag of clothes, when suddenly my Uncle Joseph appeared shouting, "Mum! Where have you been?" Seeing the clothes he grabbed them from her saying "You must be mad to worry about clothes". He had missed her from not being amongst the group of people and returned to look for her. Around them the dogs ran barking, the cattle grazed on the field, not the least disturbed by the rush and activity around them.

With the wind still south-west and calm weather conditions, the people were evacuated around 12 o'clock. Amid blue skies, the ships sailed for Nightingale with a tired and crestfallen community aboard, towing a few longboats astern. The ships reached Nightingale around three o' clock. Most of the islanders went ashore, they were going to stay in the 40 or so shacks the islanders had built when they travelled there for the guano and fatting trips.

The expatriates stayed aboard the ships, along with the sick and elderly islanders. My Granny Rose, Mabel Glass (who had just undergone an operation) were among them. Gordon Glass (Mabel's husband) stayed on board to look after them. The wind was south-west and the ships anchored in the lee of Alex Island. Ashore, the islanders sorted themselves into groups of six to 10 per hut. The men caught and killed dozens of shearwaters to cook. There was also fresh water, flour, tea, coffee, biscuits and potatoes that they had left behind from the previous fatting trip. But this would only last for a few days.

As the people ate their evening meal, they were comforted by the news that the Dutch passenger liner, MV *Tjisadane* was coming to their rescue and would be at Nightingale next morning to take the islanders to Cape Town. Although rather cramped in their small huts, the islanders slept soundly, tired out by the events of the past 48 hours. Next morning, they awoke to find the MV *Tjisadane* at anchor. After a debate concerning whether some island men should stay to see to the livestock, it was decided that all the community would go to Cape

Town on her, while the Administrator would stay behind on the MFV *Tristania 1* to await the arrival of the HMS *Leopard*.

The islanders boarded the MV *Tjisadane*, going up the rather steep, swaying, gangway. My grandfather George was among the last party to board, having had to put his dog down. He had brought the dog all the way from Tristan. He was always very fond of his dogs, as any islander will vouch for.

With the islanders settled into their cabins, which were more luxurious than their own homes, the MV *Tjisadane* sailed for Cape Town, passing Tristan on the way. The islanders stood on deck when the ship passed and stared in silence at the familiar landmarks of The Patches, Hill Piece, Herald Point and Big Beach, with the volcano still spewing out clouds of grey smoke and red chunks of hot lava. As the settlement slid from sight there were tears in many eyes. They were facing an uncertain future in a world, which none of them had seen or knew.

THE 1961 ERUPTION:
THE OUTSIDE WORLD... AND HOME AGAIN

On Monday 16th October, the MV *Tjisadane* arrived in Cape Town to cheering crowds lining the quayside. The islanders could only look on in amazement as the tugs pushed the liner against the quay. There were lots of cars, shops and other large buildings: all things they had never seen before in their lives. They were given clothes and other gifts and invited in groups to special parties. At the same time they had been told by the Administrator not to take sweets or get into cars with strangers, if asked.

London had made arrangements through the British Embassy for the MV *Stirling Castle* to bring the islanders to England, but they would have to await her arrival in four days time. They were told that they could stay on board the MV *Tjisadane* until the MV *Stirling Castle* arrived.

Although the South African Government had offered the islanders the opportunity to stay in Cape Town, they politely refused. They had only been there a few days, but had seen the buses labelled 'Blacks Only' and 'Whites Only'. They were introduced to the ugly realities of institutionalised racism for the first time and were under no illusions that if they stayed in South Africa, they would be treated as second-class citizens: in stark contrast to Tristan, where a person was (and still is) judged by their character, not by the colour of their skin. Being of the same mind, it's doubtful if the British Government would have allowed the islanders to stay in South Africa, officials from the High Commission carefully explaining their rights to them.

A week later they were on their way to England. Some were still reeling from the culture shock, having been wined, dined and entertained by the people in Cape Town. They arrived in Southampton to a cold misty land that looked rather grey under an overcast sky. The islanders were more than grateful for the kindness and the hospitality shown to them by the people of the UK. Even though they were housed in comfortable houses (the former RAF married quarters at Calshot near Southampton, after a move from an old military camp in Surrey) and had help with finding jobs, the majority still yearned to return to Tristan. However, many of the young people would have loved to stay, for England offered them better prospects and a chance to lead a more diverse lifestyle. For them, it meant the chance to live and work in a society of which they could only dream - but unfortunately, their parents did not agree with them, so they had to return home with their families.

After 18 months of expeditions and debates, the first 51 islanders left Tilbury Docks on Sunday 17th March 1963 bound for Brazil on board the mail ship, RMS *Amazon*. Led by Johnny Repetto, they transferred to the MV *Boissevain* in Rio de Janeiro and arrived on Tristan on Tuesday 9th April 1963. Sharon's Mum, Catherine, was among them, having been married several months before in England. Her dad, Stephen, and my Uncle Joseph were part of the team of 12 islanders sent to work the potato patches, tend the livestock and make the houses in the village habitable for the returning families.

Six of them worked on the fishing ships to earn enough money to pay for the passage fees for the returning islanders. My grandparents, George and Lisa, and Uncle Herbert, were part of the returning 51 islanders. I can understand why many of the islanders did not wish to stay, having lived and worked in the UK myself. In England, the pace of life is more hectic and regimented, despite all the comforts. They could not come to grips with having to lock their doors 24 hours a day; with women and children having to be careful where they walked; living with the constant fear that someone could be molested or even, murdered or raped. On Tristan, they did not have to lock their doors. Apart from working at the factory, a man was master of his own environment, free to come and go and work as he pleased. The weather dictates if it's a day at The Patches, fishing, or going to Nightingale. Life, in short, is less stressful and much more laid back. However there were a few who wished to stay in England, as they had adapted to life there much better than their fellow Islanders.

Easter Monday 1963, several weeks after the first 51 islanders returned home: the wind was from the north west, pushing quite a swell on to the boulder strewn beach. A shout went up to say that a ship was approaching the anchorage: she was going to drop off mail from the families still in England. Despite the heavy surf, the men set out to launch a small rowing dinghy. Albert Glass and Benny Green were picked to man it. The men quickly readied a wood clinker-built dinghy and pushed it down to the water's edge. Albert and Benny climbed into the dinghy and took hold of the oars. Four or five other men waited around the dinghy for Johnny Repetto, who was going to pick out a smooth time, so they could launch the dinghy.

With a shout from Johnny of "Now let her go," the men pushed the dinghy into the oncoming wave. Usually, the backwash from such a wave will help the rowers take the dinghy clear from the beach. But the unforeseen had happened. Benny and Albert pulled on their oars; the dinghy struck a huge boulder that was just under the water, causing the boat to slew across the path of the next oncoming wave. With shouts of "Look out" from the other men, Benny and Albert tried their best to bring the bow of the dinghy to face the waves, but it was struck by another wave, almost capsizing it and forcing it back on the beach, while filling it with water. With another bigger wave looming, the men ashore shouted to Benny and Albert to leave the dinghy, fearing it would capsize and trap the men beneath it. There already had been one such accident in which Anthony Rogers had crushed his leg when landing a dinghy in rough surf. He had to be sent to Cape Town for medical treatment.

With the wave about to break, both men leapt for their lives, scrambling over the slippery boulders to safety. The wave broke over the dinghy filling it with water. Caught by the current, the boat moved sluggishly seaward, until it almost reached the last line of breaking surf with just the gunwales out of the water. Watching this, my Uncle Joseph suddenly stripped to his shorts, scrambled over the boulders and plunged into the foaming surf. "Come back!" Johnny shouted, horrified, as the men watched Joseph dive underneath a breaking wave, only to appear swimming strongly on to reach the dinghy. With a heave, he climbed inside and with a couple of strokes on the oars, had the boat beyond the breaking waves.

Having bailed the dinghy as best he could, he soon reached the ship. He was given a hot shower and some clothes and the mail. On shore, the news spread through the village. My grandmother just shook her head, because she knew that Joseph was a wild one and was fearless in the face of danger and thrived on situations which lesser men would turn their backs on.

When Joseph was sighted returning from the ship, Stephen [Sharon's Dad] ran home to change into his swimming trunks. As the dinghy neared the beach, Stephen dived into the surf and swam to the dinghy. Stephen was also very daring when it came to the boats and sea. On reaching the dinghy, he climbed in and took the extra pair of oars. By now, Johnny had instructed Stephen to tell Joseph the best place to land the dinghy would be at what was left of Little Beach. Pulling strongly together, they came through the surf, using the forward momentum of the last swell to get them on to the beach where the other men grabbed the dinghy and pulled them to safety.

Both jumped out of the boat grinning at each other like schoolboys. Joseph, who was one of the strongest swimmers on Tristan, held the mailbags aloft and then passed them to Johnny, who he knew from the look on his face, was going to have some stern words with him about his rash behaviour.

On 10th November 1963, the other 185 islanders returned to Tristan aboard the Danish ferry, MV *Bornholm* (which normally plied from Copenhagen to Rønne), my parents among them. After several days of first, calm, then rough weather, all the cargo was unloaded. The crew from the MV *Tristania* helped on shore. The beach was strewn with the cargo; that which was not covered in tarpaulins was stacked in the village hall out of the weather. All people's belongings were marked with the name of the head of each house.

A day after the *Bornholm* had left, the islanders walked around the village taking stock of their surroundings. Although the volcano stood dark and threatening and smoking, where once had been green pastures, lava had now covered the two landing beaches. There was a deep feeling of fulfilment among the men. My father and Uncle Nelson had just returned from checking what needed to be done to their patches.

My mother called to them that supper was ready. They could smell the aroma of fried fish coming from the kitchen. Nelson turned to my father and said: "Come on, Spike, let's eat before the food gets cold". Despite the close proximity of the smoking volcano standing black and menacing against the evening sky (a stark reminder of how fragile their existence was on this remote Atlantic isle), with a sigh of contentment, my father replied, "It's good to be home". The birds flying overhead called to each other, seeming to echo: 'It's good to be home...'

ALL IN A DAY'S WORK

Early on a summer morning in late April, I am standing on the quay watching the MFV *Edinburgh* make her final approach to the anchorage at Tristan. The sea was very calm with the sun just rising over Big Point, casting its golden rays across the small village onto the sea beyond. All around me, the crews of the barges are getting their boats ready for the offloading. The rattling of the anchor chain as Captain Nick gives the order to drop the anchor shatters the stillness.

The first barge is already lowered into the water. "All aboard the Sandy Point Express" shouts Duncan Lavarello, the coxswain for the boat. There is a mad scramble as the stevedores, myself and the Post Master jump into the boat, each person fastening up their life jackets. Harbour regulations state that life jackets should be worn at all times.

"Mind your back, Connie," Duncan says, as he pushes the boat away from the harbour. "All ready," he says, giving us a wink with a broad grin.

A few moments later, we are alongside, waiting for the rope ladder to be thrown down, amid shouts of "Mind your head!" I am the first to scramble up the ladder. My job is to collect the diplomatic mail, and as Customs Officer, check the returning (ex-Cape Town) passengers' baggage. First I speak to the passengers and before long, their luggage is sorted. They have nothing to declare.

I next find Captain Nick. After greeting each other, we sort out the diplomatic mail. There are several bags. I check them against the numbered forms and then sign a receipt for the Captain. Next, I get the bags loaded into the barge, which by this time is almost filled with the passengers' luggage. Then I collect all passengers' passports from the Captain, and after saying goodbye, jump down into the 'Sandy Point Express', which is ready to depart from the ship.

We are soon back at the harbour, where I load the diplomatic mail into the back of the Police Land Rover. Around me, the harbour is packed with pick-ups and people as family and friends greet the passengers who have just returned from medical treatment in Cape Town. Amid the honking of car horns, I edge the Land Rover through the busy throng, and drive up the harbour road to the Administration building; there the diplomatic bags are left in charge of Cynthia Green, the Administrator's secretary.

I pass the passengers' passports on to WPC Lorraine Repetto, Executive Immigration Officer, to stamp and return to their owners, while I go to the Police Station to record my occurrence. At 09.00 I have a quick break, then follow up a report received from the vet, Dereck Rogers, that dogs have been reported worrying livestock. In this case, a few chickens have been killed and the dogs chased some cattle, which were grazing in the village.

After making investigations into the complaint, it cannot be proved which dogs killed the chickens, but the dogs which chased the cows were identified and their owners given a verbal warning to keep them under control. With the dogs having killed the chickens, I have an idea which may have been the culprits, but do not have enough evidence to support my theory. It annoys me to an extent, because people who are related through birth or marriage are not willing to tell the police anything about an incident, for fear of becoming a social outcast. All I can do is to put out a Public Notice explaining the facts.

By now the MFV *Edinburgh* has been offloaded and everyone is on lunch break. I work through what should be my break, typing up a report for the Administrator.

After lunch, I carry on with mobile patrol. I have seen a few private vehicles being driven rather recklessly through the village. After speaking to the drivers about the offence, I stop at the school at 14.00 to give a talk on road safety to the pupils, also warning a few that it is an offence to ride bicycles at night without a front light. There are some embarrassed faces amongst them. The message has been put across nicely enforced by the stern words from the then Headmistress, Marlene Swain.

After leaving the school, I visited the supermarket, to place an order for some bicycle lamps on behalf of the young offenders. The rest of the day is spent at the office compiling my reports, and e-mailing my contacts and former colleagues from training days in England, at

Hertfordshire Constabulary, to see if I can get some leaflets on road safety to pass on to the school.

At 16.30, I finish work, signing off in the occurrence book. Then it's home to change out of uniform, and get things sorted for the Youth Group children (aged from nine to 15 years). We have a Youth Club, which is held by myself, and Lorraine, once a week from 19.00 to 22.00. This week, we are having a braai (barbecue) down at the beach. The children have been busy all week collecting wood to make a bonfire. At 19.00 we meet at the school. The children are there early, waiting for Lorraine and me to arrive. As soon as we do, everyone packs their bags into the Land Rover and climbs in. Marie Repetto is there to help out, as she often does, when not working at the fishing factory.

All on board and it's about a ten minute ride to the beach at Pigbite over the solidified flow of the 1961 volcano. Once there, Lorraine and I, with the help of some of the older children, start the braai, while Marie organises a game of football rounders with the other children.

An hour later, we are finished cooking on the braai, the children gather around, Marie and Lorraine dish out lamb chops, sausages, baked beans and warm garlic bread. Soon the children are all digging in with gusto, and I pack the braai kit into the box and put it into the Land Rover. Once everyone has eaten their fill and while Marie and Lorraine put the empty tins into the bin bags, I light the bonfire. All the paper plates are thrown into the fire: soon there is a good blaze going. The children dance about it, chanting with glee! After a while it is becoming dark and the fire has burnt down; the stars shine down like thousands of glittering jewels in a cloudless sky.

To finish off the evening, I tell the children some of the legends of Tristan – of the pirates and ghosts that were said to haunt the island. Looking at their faces, I can see that they are enraptured by the story. Some glance furtively behind into the darkness, half expecting to see the bogeyman appear. By 21.30, the children are starting to yawn. With a nod to Lorraine and Marie, I announce that it is time to go back to the village. Soon we are all back into the Land Rover, having covered the embers of the fire with sand to smother it.

Then, as is customary, I drop each of the children off at their homes, but not before knowing what we have planned for the next Youth Club meeting. Maybe a fishing competition, I said. This is received with much excitement, especially from the boys, who will no doubt be planning which spot at the harbour will be the best to hold the competition and how they can have the best advantage over the girls, and I'm sure, thinking of ways to get me to agree with their plans. But Marie seems to know what they are thinking, and says before the next meeting, she and Lorraine will draw up a list of regulations to make things fair for the girls – much to the disappointment of the boys. I just grin, knowing that before next week, several of the boys will approach me with some hatched plan of their own, hoping that I will agree with them, not with what Marie and Lorraine plan, certain they will take a lot of ribbing if a girl wins the fishing competition!

A SATURDAY AT THE PATCHES

05.45 on a summer morning in mid February. I am awoken by the sound of a cockerel crowing in the field at the back of my house. My wife, Sharon, is already out of bed and getting dressed. "What's the weather like?" I ask as she pulls back the curtains.

"It looks like a nice day" she replies, opening the window and looking out. "You had better get up, if we are going to The Patches," she says. "I am off to feed the chickens and hang out the washing."

I lie in bed a few moments longer, listening to my parents speaking to Sharon. They live next door and have been up and about for some time, just returning from milking the cow. I get out of bed, dress and look out of the window. It is a lovely cloudless morning. The sun has not quite risen, the sea is fairly calm and the sky reflects a royal bluish hue over the island, with tinges of golden and yellow where the rays of sunlight shine on the horizon.

I walk downstairs, to find Sharon busy putting together a packed lunch of tea, sandwiches, chocolates, apples and soft drinks for us to take to The Patches. She has already finished her other chores and looks up as I walk into the kitchen. "Is Leon ready yet?" she asks. "Yes," I reply, smiling at thoughts of Leon's comments about going to The Patches. Leon is our son and (at the time of writing) has just returned from IT training in England. He thinks the grass is much greener there, hence his comments about The Patches: "I will be glad when this bloody work at The Patches is finished. What a boring life style. Work, work, every weekend. No break at all. I can't wait to get off this place."

Well I can't say that I blame him. I felt much the same when I was his age (20 years old, then). But there are people on Tristan who would not agree with Leon and enjoy the life they live here. I can understand their point of view as well. After all, we are all born with different outlooks, skills and interests in life. Leon has already spent three and half years at college in the UK since he left school here five years ago: two years at Denstone College near Uttoxeter in Staffordshire and another at an IT College at Dudley in the West Midlands.

The Denstone connection with Tristan came about in 1982 when the President and Chairman of the Tristan da Cunha Association, Michael Swales, at that time a House Master at the school and a former member of the 1955 Cambridge Expedition to Gough Island, led a group of the college's students on another Tristan expedition, this time to Inaccessible Island. They surveyed it and collected data on the flora and fauna. The project went so well that Michael arranged for students from Tristan to undertake a two year scholarship at Denstone studying for their GCSE's (an English schools examination undertaken at 16). This has now ceased for financial reasons; my son was the last Tristanian student to participate.

I have a quick cuppa then get the Land Rover out of the garage, hook up the trailer and throw the bags for digging into it.

By now, everyone is just about ready to set off three and a half miles to The Patches. My father has been ready for half an hour and is standing impatiently by the Land Rover waiting for the rest of the family to put their gear into the back. "Hurry up," he says. "We haven't got all day."

"Don't panic, a few moments shan't make much difference in getting to The Patches" I answer. But he is not convinced. He belongs to the older generation of Tristanians who lived by the motto "make hay while the sun shines". It was frowned upon if people arrived late at The Patches to do a day's work. I remember my grandfather telling me that in his day, the men used to be at The Patches before daybreak, waiting until it was light enough to start work.

Even the dogs are aware we are leaving the village and run about barking, eager to be away. Just then Jack Green (my cousin, who lives next door) drives past in his pickup en route to The Patches with his family. I follow suit, shouting to Leon not to forget to collect his grandmother (my mother-in-law) at her home in his Jeep. Leon just nods as he walks to the driver's seat, cigarette in hand. Smoking is one of the vices he picked up while in England and is something his mother and I disapprove of, as neither of us smokes.

About a quarter mile outside the village, we see other families going to The Patches in their pickups and Land Rovers, several ahead, others following. Seven minutes later we arrive, to find Jack getting the scrapers and buckets from one of the huts. Jack and I share the work in our patches, either planting or harvesting the potatoes. Most island families do the same. Our fathers worked their patches together for more than 50 years.

A scraper is the tool used by the islanders to dig their potatoes. It is made from a garden fork, by bending the prongs of the fork at a right angle, and putting in another handle which is about a metre long. To dig the potatoes, one stands about a metre away from the row and hits down with a chopping motion to the drill (the drill is the hollow between the rows of potatoes, about 36cm in width). The prongs of the scraper enter the soil about 12cm in depth. Then the scraper is pulled towards you levelling out the soil of the row, so uncovering the potatoes.

The potatoes are picked up by the person with the scraper and chucked into a heap to dry. A heap is a hollow area of soil about a metre square, into which the potatoes are thrown after being dug. Four rows of potatoes are dug which is called a 'tear' then a new heap is made. This continues until the whole patch has been dug out. These heaps allow the potatoes to dry thus giving the women better access when choosing seed potatoes for next year and to sort the others into different sizes, before emptying them into the bags.

The method used by the women when gathering up the potatoes is to first pick out the seed potatoes, which tend to be of medium size. Then, they sort the others into two sizes: large and small. What's left in the heap will be the potatoes that have been cut by the prong of the scraper and the very small ones. These will be gathered last and used to feed cows, ducks and chickens. The potatoes are picked up in a two gallon (10 litre) bucket. The buckets are filled level, then dumped into a bag. It takes four buckets to fill one and a half bushels (about 50 kilos) of potatoes.

The bags are left in the patch to be collected by the men when they are ready to load them on to the vehicles to take them back to the village. The seed potatoes are left in the huts built at The Patches.

They are either stored in plastic trays or wire crates, to prevent the rats getting at them. They will remain there until next year when they have sprouted enough to be planted. The average size of the patches is about four metres wide and 14 metres long. The process of working is that both men and women will help with the digging until it's threequarters finished. Then the women will leave off digging and sort the potatoes, while the men finish off, then move onto the next patch.

This will carry on until all the patches for the day have been dug. Usually we will dig about four to six on a Saturday starting, at 06.00 and getting finished around 12.30. Often we will take half a day's leave or go down at 15.30 after work and dig out several patches, because sometimes we get almost a week of rain, even during the summer. In the past, before the islanders were employed by the Government and the Fish Factory, they used to bring the harvest home in wooden carts pulled by oxen. Then it became possible to use the Government tractors. As there were only three, it meant waiting at times on a Saturday until 17.00 for a tractor, although we had finished digging at midday. Since the islanders have been able to afford to purchase their own vehicles, life is more flexible when working at The Patches. However the downside is that people are not as fit as they used to be, because they don't walk there to do a day's work.

When digging, there is not much talking taking place, as it's a very physical task. Most of the conversation is about this year's harvest, arrival of the ship with cargo, fishing, or an item of news seen on the TV. Sometimes there is a competition to see who digs the biggest potato. We will have to watch Jack, as he's usually up to his antics trying to get the biggest spud to put in his heap, claiming he dug it.

After digging a few patches the whole family sits down for a picnic lunch laughing and talking to other people who are passing by. Someone shouts: "Hey sonny, looks like you're hungry." Jack answers, "No I'm not, would you like a nibble?" His friend calls back, "Thanks, I have already eaten, but it appears you have got big woodies." (Tristan slang for large potatoes). Jack replies, "They're not too bad - much better than last year."

My father stands up, grabs a couple of scrapers and a few empty sacks and heads off towards the next patch, walking precariously on top of a stone wall, saying to no one in particular: "Come on, we still have another patch to dig." Leon looks up from eating his sandwich and retorts, "Where's Cliff Hanger off to now?" referring more to his grandfather trying to keep his balance on top of the wall, than to him going to dig another patch of potatoes. In all we have to work in 58 patches of different sizes each year. Some are for members of the family who live on their own. My family include Sharon, Leon, my parents Edwin and Monica, my sister Sheila, and her son Warren, Sharon's Mum Catherine and her Aunt Gracie. Jack's family are Cynthia his wife; Shane, his son; and his mother, Winnie. Jack's mum and mine are sisters.

11.45: we are finished digging for the day. While the women put the scrapers and buckets away, the men tie up the sacks of potatoes and carry them from the patch to load onto the pickup and the Land Rover's trailer. We have to drive to a couple of different locations to collect the spuds from where we have dug. Soon the family is in the vehicles headed back home. When we reach there, the men unload the sacks, carrying them into the potato huts built next to our houses. To identify which sack comes from which patch, they are tied with different coloured string or flax. We will harvest 70 to 50 bushels of potatoes on a Saturday if the weather is good. Most families will have a total of 150 to 100 bushels each year, depending how the crop has grown.

Digging is a very dusty job and the women always have loads of washing at the end of the day. The families in each group take it in turn each weekend to provide refreshments. It's a time to relax together on the lawn, planning for the next weekend, discussing if any patches need to be dug during the week.

Later that day I return my parents to The Patches in the Land Rover. They will spend the weekend there at their camping hut. The camping huts are about 10 metres long and four metres wide. They have modest facilities: kitchen, bedroom, living room and toilet, similar to what one would find in a mountain hut.

My father will either tend his vegetable plot or go fishing from the beach with a hand line. Most families have camping huts built at The Patches, where they spend weekends, Easter and Christmas Holidays.

A ROCKHOPPER COPPER AT WORK: CONSERVATION PATROL AND POLICING THE PENGUINS

I first got involved with conservation work soon after joining the Police in 1987. It was mostly helping Jim Kerr, the Education Officer at that time (who's now returned as Education Advisor), monitor a school project. This was checking a yellow nosed albatross colony on the base of the mountain overlooking the village. Jim and I would take the eldest pupils from St Mary's School on field trips up the mountain, to ring and count these birds, as part of their Tristan Studies lessons. In 1992, with help from John Cooper and Peter Ryan from the Percy Fitzpatrick Institute of Cape Town, I started an annual census of bird colonies and the fur seals at different sites on Tristan. This expanded over the years, with me going on field trips to Nightingale and Gough Island. This is still a continuing project involving me and Trevor Glass, the Head of Tristan Conservation Department.

Here are some sample narratives from our early field trips:
Friday 25 September 1992: with the help of Special PC Clive Glass, I counted the penguin rookery at Jew's Point. It was a nice sunny day and we took our small dinghy, *Stormy*, with its outboard motor, the two miles to the Point. After landing safely, we spent an hour counting the penguins. They were found to have two eggs in the nest and there were a few nests without any eggs. We took eggs from the nests that had two and put them into the empty ones. A total of 357 pairs were counted.
Wednesday 7 October 1992: with the wind light south-east, Clive and I left for The Caves to count the penguin rookeries at Trypot and Goat Road Gulch, which is about three and a half miles from The Caves, past Stony Beach. Again we travelled using our small dinghy

with the outboard motor. While there, a count was made of the fur seals, of which there were 40. Next day we set off at 06.30 to count the rookeries at Trypot and Goat Road Gulch. To reach the penguin rookeries we had to cross a very narrow stretch of beach, with the sea in places at the foot of the cliffs, which rises sheer to about 3,000 feet. Luckily the weather was in our favour and apart from getting wet, the task was carried out successfully. During the journey we counted two elephant seals, a male and a female. The male was about 18 foot in length and the female about ten foot in length. At the penguin rookery at Trypot we counted 734 pairs. There were also eight yellow nosed albatrosses nesting nearby. At Goat Road Gulch we counted a total of 412 pairs, 30 of which had their nests made in the bottom of the Gulch, thus a flood would destroy them.

Friday 9 October 1992: we left The Caves at 06.30 by dinghy. Just after setting off, we had to turn back to replace the propeller shear pin on the outboard motor. Our only spare shear pin was crudely made from a 4-inch nail. The wind was very strong, 35 to 40 knots, from east north east. Clive had to sit in the bow of the dinghy with the spare food and dogs to keep the bow of the dinghy from being blown about. I could see each gust of wind approaching, whipping the sea with swirling white eddies of water. Fortunately the sea was not rough and we were able to keep close to the shore until we rounded Anchorstock Point. Half a mile off shore we saw a yacht under close-reefed sails running before the wind. We encountered a heavy north east swell, with waves higher than a two-storey house, the larger ones rippling on the crest, threatening to break over into the dinghy. I was still keeping close to the shoreline, but on Clive's suggestion I steered more off-shore, manoeuvring the dinghy between the heavy swell on the smoother sections of the sea. I winked at Clive as I raced out of the way of a looming wave. Clive grinned and shouted: "The dinghy is riding much better than our fishing boat. It's more movable."

Giving Herald Point a wide berth, we hove to off the harbour. This should prove interesting, I thought, as we watched the swell breaking through the entrance. Several men were on the harbour, Herbert standing clear, called us in between the sets of waves. With a deft wave of his arm he beckoned to come. I steadily increased to maximum revs so not to shear the propeller pin by a sudden burst of speed. Ronald, who was on the harbour, gesticulated with his hand as I slowed down the boats. Out of the corner of my eye I saw a large wave looming, and knew that if I did not slow down, the wave would catch the boat at the point where it would break over the stern. This could mean the dinghy being swamped or capsized; at the mercy of the wave and my not being in control of the situation. I prevented this by slowing down and allowing the wave to pass, then increasing the speed of the motor using the forward momentum of the wave to ride on its back. As it broke and flattened, the dinghy surfed through the wave into the calm waters of the harbour, with Clive grinning from ear to ear with the thrill of the ride.

Monday 26 October 1992: Clive and I left for Sandy Point by dinghy, to count the penguins there. On arrival we were unable to land, due to a heavy surf. I swam ashore and counted. The rookery at the east end had 500 pairs; Phoenix Beach 120 pairs; Big Gulch 558 pairs. About half the number of each rookery had already hatched with one or two chicks to a nest. The male penguins had also returned to the rookeries. During 25 September and 4-7 October, only the female birds were at the rookeries. There were nine cattle and six sheep grazing at Sandy Point. The grass is long enough to graze another 20 cattle and it would help the pasture around the village and out west if that amount of livestock could be taken to Sandy Point. At 15.00, I returned to the beach and swam to the dinghy. We arrived back at the harbour at 16.45.

Friday 29 December 1993: at 07.00, Clive and I set off to count the rookeries at Trypot, Goat Road Gulch, East End, Sandy Point, Phoenix Beach, Big Gulch and Jew's Point, accompanied by Herbert Glass and Adrian Swain, as Clive was taking an 11 month calf to graze on the pastures of Sandy Point. On arrival at Sandy Point, we could not land because of a heavy surf breaking on the beach. Luckily for us, Joe Green was there with the launch, *Atlantic Spray*, having taken some people to pick plums from the trees growing there. We tied the dinghy alongside the launch then tipped the calf into the sea, where it swam ashore. Clive, Herbert and Adrian landed the dinghy at Big Gulch, while Joe offered to take me down to Trypot and Goat Road Gulch.

On rounding the reef at Sandy Point, we saw the heavy swell from the south that had caused the surf at Sandy Point was much worse the closer we got to Trypot, causing the reef to break across the bay. Joe pointed out that it would be dangerous to swim ashore because of the distance over which the reef was breaking from the beach. We returned to Sandy Point where I was able to swim ashore and count the rookeries at East End and Sandy Point. Clive and I decided to count the young penguins as some of the adults may have left. It was easy to count them as they stood apart from the adults in groups of six or eight, some still had downy feathers.

I counted 140 young and returned to Sandy Point and swam to the dinghy where the others were waiting. We then set off for Jew's Point. Herbert, Adrian and Clive had counted 217 young penguins at Big Gulch and 93 young at Phoenix Beach. Arriving at Jew's Point, I swam ashore and counted only 20 young penguins in the Rookery.

Tuesday 11 January 1994: it was a 'Nightingale' day and a fishing day. Trevor Glass and I set off to finish counting the penguins and fur seals at the Caves. We counted 200 fur seals and 50 young seal pups. With the weather starting to get worse, we headed for Stony Beach where it was nice and smooth, so I waded ashore from the dinghy and walked about a mile along the beach to the Rookeries. Nearby, where I had waded ashore, was a young elephant seal, about five feet in length, basking in the sun. On reaching Goat Road Gulch, I counted 30 fur seals on the beach. In the rookery there were only three young penguins and 100 adults. The rookery at Trypot had 24 young penguins and 170 adult penguins, not a successful count at all. On reaching the dinghy, I saw the reason why. About 30 feet away, was a young penguin in the water swimming out to sea. I determined that this year, I will try to get the penguins counted between October and November. I know for a fact that the penguins first lay their eggs at Jew's Point a week or two before the other rookeries on Tristan.

On the trip back to the harbour, we had the bad luck to break the pin on the prop of the outboard, then forgetting to change over petrol tanks. It took about ten minutes to replace the pin on the outboard and swap the empty tank for the full one. Amidst driving rain and a 25 knot head wind we arrived at the harbour approximately 16.00 to find most of the fishing boats already back.

Tuesday 21 November 1995: with the wind light south east, although the sky was very overcast with a slight drizzle falling, the boats were out fishing and at 07.15, Jimmy Glass and I decided that the weather was suitable to complete the penguin census for this year. We liaised with Joe Green who would drive the RIB *Wave Dancer*. Jimmy thought it would be quicker to use wet suits to swim the short distance from the boat to the beach at each of the rookeries instead of using a small dinghy. At 09.00 we left the harbour and headed east to Jew's Point, the first rookery on the route. At 09.20 we arrived and slipped into our wet suits. Joe circled for several minutes until he caught the right set of waves, then got in as close as possible to the beach. We then leapt into the surf and swam six metres or so to the beach. Upon reaching it, we found our notebooks had become wet. The plastic bags, in which they were wrapped, had sprung a leak.

Because the adult penguins were no longer sitting on the nests, we counted the baby penguins instead. They stood apart from the adult birds in clichés of ten or 20, some standing almost as tall as their parents, but all covered in the same fluffy coat. A total of 183 young penguins were counted, amounting to the presence of 366 adult penguins. Taking into account the egg loss during the incubation period and death of the penguin chicks due to the skuas and rats, (or from poaching, as this rookery is only about two miles from the village), this was not a bad start. Five dead chicks were observed. Last year Jimmy and Clive counted the penguins in September and counted a total of 459 pairs. At 10.15 we swam back to the boat and continued on to the rookery at Big Gulch.

At 10.30 we arrived at Big Gulch and swam ashore after waiting for the right set of waves. Jimmy counted the bottom rookeries in the Big Gulch while I counted the top rookery. The penguins in the top rookery had extended the nesting site right up past the top edge of the bottom cliff in the gulch. At the top rookery, it's quite difficult to count the young penguins, because the nesting site is situated on an old rock fall. The young chicks there are in clichés of five and eight amongst the rock, and between 20 to 30 in the open areas to prevent the clichés scuttling off under the crevice of the nearest rock. I had to creep silently up on each cliché following the sounds of their chirping, take a head count, then move on without them being aware of my presence. Several clichés were alerted by the adults and scurried off under the rocks; I had to poke amongst them with a stick to get them counted. Jimmy had completed the bottom rookeries, which were on open ground and shouted that he would go and count the rookery at Phoenix Beach, which is only about 200 metres east of the Big Gulch rookery. A total of 733 young penguins were counted, amounting to again, the presence of 1,466 adult birds. One dead chick was observed. We found a sheep in the Big Gulch with an orange tag in the right ear, but no earmark. This animal had been there for quite some time, judging by the area it had been grazing. This sheep had come from a flock, which is at Halfway Beach, one mile west of the Big Gulch. It had got there by walking along the beach. The owners had been warned to get them out of Big Gulch area.

At 11.30, I finished at the Big Gulch and walked to Phoenix Beach. Jimmy was waiting there for me, having counted 149 young penguins; the presence of 298 adult birds was noted. At 11.45, we walked one mile across Sandy Point to the rookery at East End arriving at midday. A total of 509 young penguins were counted to the presence of 1,018 adult birds, five bad eggs were found in the bottom of the gulch. At 12.30 we swam back to the boat and headed to Trypot and Goat Road Gulch arriving there at 12.45. I swam ashore at Trypot and counted the penguins while Jimmy swam ashore at Goat Road Gulch. There was much heavier surf breaking so it took longer to choose the right moment to swim ashore.

The penguins at Trypot are on quite open ground but several rookeries are in a small gully. When approached, the cliché in the bottom rookery will rush off to the cliché in the rookery above, until they reach the top of the gully. There I found a mass of bodies, two or three deep, as if a scrum was formed for a rugby match, so I became the ref and waded in to get a head count. The total of 140 young penguins were counted, a presence of 820 adult birds. One penguin was observed still sitting on two eggs, while the yellow nosed albatrosses had increased from 17 to 20, also being joined by a sooty albatross.

14.20: I swam back to the boat. As I came near, Jimmy, who had already arrived, threw me a rope and started to give me a pull. At that moment he told Joe to move the RIB into deeper water as they had drifted on top of a reef. Suddenly I found myself dragged along at an alarming speed. Despite my best efforts to do some surfing I ended up swallowing gallons of the South Atlantic and had to let go. I surfaced, spitting out water to hear gales of laughter from Jimmy. I swam to the boat quite convinced that this was another of James' practical jokes, as he had arrived 10 minutes earlier and plotted the whole thing. Jimmy counted 297 young penguins at Goat Road Gulch; the presence of 594 adult birds noted.

14.25: we set off for The Caves, on the way encountering quite a heavy swell and breeze from the south. At 15.00 we reached, but could not land in the 'Pond' (an area of water adjacent to the site, where small boats can moor) so we went to the 'Old Landing Place'. After two attempts to land, we swam ashore and collected some coils of 20 mm rope. With the breeze increasing, we did not stay to count the seals, of which there seemed several hundred on the beach. We left The Caves at 15.25 and had a good run back to the harbour with leading wind and waves, arriving back at 15.50.

AN ENVIRONMENTAL INSPECTION ON GOUGH ISLAND:

On 3rd November 1997 I left Tristan on board the South African National Antarctic Programme's vessel, SA *Agulhas*, to carry out the annual conservation inspection at Gough Island, which is 220 miles from our main island. Gough is uninhabited except for a group of South African meteorologists, who spend a year there before being replaced by new people, courtesy of the ship's annual visit.

The SA *Agulhas* arrived at Gough Island the next day at 15.30 and anchored off the Old Glen. The first flight by helicopter was at 16.15, which consisted of two Tristan Public Works Department personnel; three DEAT (Department for Environmental Affairs and Tourism) personnel; the ship's doctor; Onno Huyser (the Environmental inspector); Sam Oosthuizen (voyage co-coordinator) and myself as Conservation Officer. Gough Meteorological Team 42 was at the helipad to greet us. All had grown their hair and beards long during the year they had spent on Gough, resembling characters from Huckleberry Finn. The leader of Gough Team 42 gave us an inspection tour of the meteorological station and other buildings. The area around the base and buildings was found to be clean and tidy. It was obvious that Team 42 had been conservation and environmentally conscientious throughout the year by the appearance of the station and the surrounding area. During this time, the helicopter was busy off-loading the year's supplies for the new meteorological team. That evening, a meeting was held by the coordinator and the team leaders of Gough 42 and 43 to introduce the new arrivals and explain regulations governing the base, with special emphasis placed on the drawing of blinds to prevent bird strikes.The offloading by helicopters was completed at 10.00 on 7th November; the SA *Agulhas* then sailed for Cape Town.

I was given the initiation on Gough along with the other new members. One had to do a handstand with someone holding your legs, while someone else held a pint mug of beer. The trick is to drink it upside down without spilling any. I think most of us spilt more than we drank!

The PWD teams and the Met teams worked almost around the clock to complete repairs, maintenance and installations to the site. The SA Air Force helicopter personnel chipped in, helping with the work, even taking turns as kitchen skivvies. A new helipad was erected out of stainless steel to replace the old one. This platform was constructed out of 10 cm stainless steel pipes driven into the ground as piles, held in place by aluminum scaffolding. The platform is about two metres high and can support four 2,700 litre plastic barrels of water.

A new generator and two new Perkins diesel water-cooled engines were installed to replace the old ones. There appeared to be no oil leaks from the engines. General maintenance was carried out on the crane and electrical systems around the station. 40,000 litres of Polar diesel was pumped ashore from the SA *Agulhas* to keep the engines running for a year. The fuel tanks were checked and no fuel leaks were seen. The green vegetation growing around and under the fuel tanks proved it. All waste, such as left over stores, crushed metal tins and old photographic chemicals, were packed into old wooden boxes then placed into metal containers. Some were shipped on the SA *Agulhas*, the rest were shipped on another vessel, the SA *Outeniqua*. This ship was to collect us from Gough.

All left over poultry products were burnt in the incinerator to prevent avian diseases. All left over food that was not burnt was tipped daily down the (skivvyget) kitchen midden. (This is a hole that goes into the sea about six metres across by 15 metres deep. The sewage also runs into this hole). All paper, cardboard, wood and alien plants such as milk thistle (*sonchus oleraceus*), large leaf dock (*rumex obtusifolius*) were weeded out by Team 42 during this year around the station, but docks are so widely spread over the island they are impossible to get rid off. No potato plants were seen around the station.

The yellow nosed albatross colony was monitored by Onno Huyster who with the help of Pete (the old team medic) and myself. The updated information on the colony was filled onto a more detailed map of the colony. Several unmarked nesting sites on which the birds had already been ringed were marked onto the map. A check was also made on the penguin rookery at Seal Beach. It was noted that the penguins had not hatched any of their eggs. I found this to be a bit surprising as on Tristan, Nightingale and Inaccessible, the penguin chicks are about four weeks old. This showed that the penguins at Gough Island laid their eggs about the first week in October.

Great care was taken to examine all fresh fruit and vegetables brought ashore. They were found to be in good condition except several of the tomatoes, which had fungus growing from the core. These were disposed off. The list of vegetables and fruit were potatoes, carrots, pumpkins, squash, onions, garlic bulbs and cucumber, tomatoes, apples, oranges, naarjities and pears.

There are mice on Gough, but no sign of them in or around the station; only on walks did I observe a few. The members of the old team recorded having caught and killed 591 mice during the year. [Editor's note: the population of mice has since increased dramatically; they eat alive the chicks of the Tristan albatross and threaten the very survival of this globally-significant species].

FISHING INSPECTIONS: On Monday 10th November 1997 at 16.30, I went on board the MFV *Edinburgh* where I spent three days observing the method of fishing. I was hoisted by crane (which had just been fixed)! Standing on the outer edge of an octagonal platform to a small fishing boat, bobbing about 50 metres on the sea below, I hung on for dear life to the netting of the platform as it swung alarmingly to and fro; fortunately I was able to scramble safely into the boat, my dignity intact.

The MFV *Edinburgh* was fishing from The Glen to Isolda Rock on the south face of Gough Island. The captain was using 14 lines, with 20 traps per line, fishing at an average depth of 50 metres and about 25 metres from shore. There were four powerboats, each carrying between 25 and 30 traps. Several soldier fish (*sebastes cupensis*) caught in the traps when the lines were hauled were used as bait for the traps.

Catches of crayfish recorded on the 11th, 12th and 13th of November are as follows: Tuesday 11th November 1997, total weight of fish caught 1,252 kg (the powerboats caught 485 kg): whole raw, packed four cases; tails, packed 64 cases; whole cooked, packed 34 cases. Wednesday 12th November 1997, total weight of fish caught 1,012 kg; (the powerboats caught 479 kg); whole cooked packed 35 cases; whole raw packed four cases; tails packed 53 cases; Thursday 14th November 1997: total weight of fish caught 1,377 kg (powerboats caught 428 kg); tails packed 101 cases.

A total of 617 cases of fish were put on board the SA *Agulhas* between 21.00 and 00.00 on 7th November 1997; 3,366 cases were put on board the SAS *Outeniqua* on 14th November 1997. Of these, there were 3,067 whole raw and cooked and 299 tails. Left on board the MFV *Edinburgh* were 4,272 cases of whole cooked and raw, 1,116 cases of tails and 138 cases of octopus.

The average length of crayfish measured 87 mm to 98 mm. Very few undersized fish were caught; none was found when I checked. The average weight caught per line was 120 kg. The captain and crew of the MFV *Edinburgh* were very conservation minded, keeping the lights dimmed to prevent bird strikes and not throwing any litter over the side of the ship.

A senior officer from the SAAF told Onno Huyster and myself that several of the SA *Agulhas*' crew had caught a large number of white fish to take back to Cape Town to sell. There was also a mention that some of them had brought small chest freezers to store fish in for that purpose. The environmental officer had informed the captain of the

SA *Agulhas* that white fish could only be caught for consumption on board the ship and no five-finger to be taken under 250 mm.

The radio operator from the old team said there was no sighting of any poachers during the year.

There was a large peat slip at the edge of the cliff about 20 metres west of the crane. This peat slip caused quite a bit of damage, by destroying almost the entire catwalk, which the team uses as a means to get to the observation platform, from which instructions are passed to the crane driver. The peat slip is about 25 metres wide and 3.5 metres high. I spoke to the co-coordinator and head of Public Works Department about preventing the slip deteriorating any further. Suggestions were made to try and shore up its face, or that the DEAT should get a geologist to check it out next year, as there may be a danger if left unchecked. Some of the nearer buildings could indeed fall into the sea.

I would like to thank Gough Teams 42 and 43, the co-coordinator Sam Oosthuizen, the DEAT team, Onno Huyster, the PWD team, the Air Force personnel, Nick de Plessis (Captain of the MFV *Edinburgh*) for all the information and support they gave towards compiling this report and making my stay at Gough a pleasant one. At 17.00 on the 14th November we were air lifted on board and sailed for Tristan, arriving early on 16th November.

A FISHING DAY: Tuesday 3rd November 1998 – Mike Batty, Gerald Rogers, Allan Swain and I took the *Wave Dancer* to sample fish and continue the penguin census. We set off at 10.00 to Stony Beach where we carried out fishery work until 14.30. Mike and Allan then put Gerald and I ashore at Halfway Beach where we walked to Big Gulch to count the penguins. Gerald counted the bottom rookeries while I counted the top ones. A total of 1,086 chicks were counted to the presence of 2,172 adults. This rookery had improved since the last census.

By 14.00 Gerald and I were finished and walked back to Halfway Beach. On arrival, we found that the swell had increased somewhat, but thanks to Mike and Allan, who on timing it just right, put the bow of the *Wave Dancer* on to the beach while we scrambled into the boat getting quite wet in the process. At 16.40 we arrived back at the harbour before the fishing boats.

FINISHING THE PENGUIN CENSUS: Monday 16th November 1998: I decided to finish the penguin census. Accompanied by Simon Glass and Gerald Rogers, we set off in the *Wave Dancer* at 10.50. We had planned to land at The Pond by The Caves, but a heavy swell prevented this, so we motored on to Stony Beach Bay. I put Simon and Gerald ashore, getting them quite wet after deciding not to run the *Wave Dancer* on to the beach, because the boulders were too big and would damage the hull. Simon and Gerald set off to count the rookeries at Stony Hill and Stony Beach, where they counted a total of 639 chicks to the presence of 1,278 adults. They arrived back at the boat at 15.00. I picked them up again by putting the bow of the boat on to the beach between sets of waves; both got wet again but seemed to enjoy it! By 16.00, we were back at the harbour.

Due to the fact the rookeries at Trypot and Goat Road Gulch are quite inaccessible, because of the weather, making a census is a dangerous task. Jimmy and I will count those rookeries every five years because we have no fear of any poaching in these areas. Penguin census for 1998: (numbers of penguins counted compared to 1995 census): -

Rookery	Census 1995	Census 1998
Jew's Point	183 Chicks/366 Adults	414 Chicks/ 828 Adults
		[An increase of 462 pairs]
Big Gulch	733 Chicks/1,466 Adults	1,086 Chicks/2,172 Adults
		[An increase of 706 pairs]
Phoenix Beach	149 Chicks/298 Adults	309 Chicks/618 Adults
		[An increase of 329 pairs]
East End Sandy Point	509 Chicks/1,018 Adults	571 Chicks/1,142 Adults
		[An increase of 124 pairs]
Stony Beach & Stony Hill	587 Chicks/1,174 Adults	639 Chicks/1,278 Adults
		[Total increase since 1995 of 1,621 pairs]
Trypot & Goat Road Gulch Census Combined	707 Chicks/1, 414 Adults	[Not counted this year]
Grand Totals:	5,736	6,038
(Trypot & Goat Road not counted)		[An increase of 302]

There is a marked increase in the penguin rookeries at Tristan. It seems the conservation work we carry out is well worth our efforts.

One of the reasons conservation work is carried out on this scale on the Tristan group of islands is because people around the world are now taking more of an interest in conservation work led by such groups as Greenpeace, who campaign for the protection of birds and mammals all over the world. Just because Tristan da Cunha is remote, it hasn't escaped the scrutiny of the conservationist. There is ever increasing pressure from London to monitor the wild life on all South Atlantic Islands belonging to the UK. The reason is that wanton killing of the yellow nosed albatrosses by Japanese fishing vessels, using long-lines, has caused an uproar in London, so the British Government is demanding more protection for these birds on the Tristan da Cunha group of islands.

A special group has been formed to help raise awareness of the importance of this task. They are called the United Kingdom Overseas Territories Conservation Forum (www.ukotcf.org). The Royal Society for the Protection of Birds (www.rspb.org.uk) has put huge resources, with dedicated personnel resident on the island, into this conservation work and much else on Tristan. I have personally raised concerns about invasive species, such as mice and rats, with the UK Ministers responsible for Overseas Territories at the annual conference organised by the Foreign and Commonwealth Office in London of the chief ministers of the UK Overseas Territories, emphasising the threat from these so-called 'supermice' to the Tristan Albatross.

Therefore, it is better seen we are capable of looking after and controlling our own wildlife needs for the future without having this imposed from the UK. This needs the help of all concerned to carry out this task. It's in our best interest to conserve our wildlife for future generations of young Tristanians. After all the islanders have been living in harmony with nature since the first settlers (including my ancestor, William Glass). Let's hope it will continue to be that way in the future.

Back on the first longboat trip to Nightingale, I made plans with all government employees to do a spot of road clearing once they had finished their own personal work. It was arranged that Allan Swain and Herbert Glass would take charge of a gang of nine men. They would work from 09.00 to 15.00, without a lunch break. I provided the refreshments for them. The men worked for two days on Friday 25th and Saturday 26th February 2000 to clear the section of the road I had asked them to. The only tools they had to work with were one spade, one pick, two axes and two short lengths of rope. Only a few men had gloves. The rest worked with their bare hands, breaking the edges of the tussock and pulling up the young plants.

I am pleased to say that everyone worked very hard to finish the job as we had expected the German cruise liner, MS *Bremen*, to arrive soon the following week. The area cleared was the top half of the main road, continuing to where the paths parted for the first and second ponds, until the wood was reached. The west road was cleared from the landing to the path that joins the main road. Everyone on Nightingale made a conscious effort to keep the place tidy.

On the Friday, while work on the road was in progress, Neil and I carried out a census of the yellow nosed albatross chicks nesting near the ponds and the woods leading to them. The results were: first pond,160 chicks counted on the nests; second pond, 323 chicks counted on the nests; third pond, 164 chicks counted on the nests. One chick was observed nesting in the west end of the third pond with a crooked beak and a deformed right wing. I was not sure that he would be able to fly when the time came for him to leave the nest; 70 chicks were counted in the woods that lead to the second pond, and 40 chicks were counted in the wood that leads to the first pond. Several bits of flax were found growing in this wood and the first pond. This flax will have to be destroyed, as it's an alien plant on Nightingale.

PENGUIN AND FUR SEAL CENSUS AT THE CAVES AND STONY BEACH 2001: on Wednesday 31st October 2001, while on holiday at The Caves, I decided to carry out a census of the Penguin Rookeries at Stony Beach. My wife Sharon and I set off from The Caves at 10.00 and arrived at Stony Beach at 11.30. We had to cross a narrow stretch of beach where at times the waves reached the foot of the cliff. We managed to get across without getting wet, judging the right set of waves, before making a dash to the wider section of the beach. By 11.30 we had arrived at Stony Beach. I counted the penguin rookery at the bay there first. There were 354 penguins sitting on their nests, 50 of them were sitting on eggs that still had not hatched. Of about half of the penguins that had baby chicks, about 100 of these had hatched two. But it was clear to see that the penguins, which were only feeding one chick, had bigger penguin chicks. A penguin will often hatch two eggs but will only raise one chick. Forty eggs were found broken a couple of metres from the rookery, the work of skuas or rats.

I next counted the penguins' rookeries on Stony Hill. This is a volcano similar in appearance to the 1961 volcano at the village, although Stony Hill is around 300 years older. An interesting fact is that both volcanoes lie almost in a straight line to each other, on opposite sides of the island, north-east to south-west. Counting the penguins on Stony Hill proved to be a more arduous task, because most of the penguins had their nests made in small nooks and crannies of the volcano. I had to poke about with a stick to get an accurate head count.

The Rockhopper Penguin is a most disagreeable bird and was always ready to have a go at his neighbour, the world and myself in general. Almost all of the rookery could be held on charge for breach of the peace!

In all I counted 420 penguins on the nests, about 350 with chicks; the rest were sitting on unhatched eggs. The top penguin rookery on Stony Hill had only 40 penguins in it, 30 of these had chicks. The cattle at Stony Beach graze next to this rookery. This may cause the penguins to move to other rookeries around Tristan. At 14.00, I finished the penguin census and we set off back to The Caves arriving there at 16.00. This time, luck was with us, because we crossed the narrow beach at low tide, despite the swell having increased.

A further holiday task - on Thursday 1st November, I counted the fur seals on the Cave Point, and the total amounted to 344. While there, we saw two whales in Dead Man's Bay, about five hundred metres off shore. These appeared to be the Southern Right Whale. Each was about 15 metres in length. The next day at 08.30, I saw an elephant seal about five metres from the beach, about four metres in length. At this time, Neil and Mark Swain arrived with the RIB to pick us up. We left The Caves at 10.15 and arrived back at the harbour at 11.00 hours. During our time at The Caves, I was in contact with Captain Nick on the MFV *Kelso* by VHF radio, Captain Nick had daily contact with Tristan Radio, so we didn't feel completely cut off from civilization.

A DAY ON THE MOUNTAIN HERDING SHEEP

It is 01.00 hours on a November morning. The wind is from the southwest with hardly a whisper of breeze about. The stars are very bright. They seem to be much closer than usual and there are a few clouds about, mostly in the east. A pale waning moon on its last quarter casts an eerie glow over the island throwing deep shadows on the face of the mountain. I am standing at the bottom of the garden with James, waiting for Jack to get ready. After waiting a couple of weeks, we finally have good weather to go up the mountain to check on our sheep. Jack appears, so we climb on to our motorbikes and set off down to meet the rest of our gang, waiting at Gary's house. There are ten of us; we have all taken sheep up on the mountain to breed. Working as a group makes life much easier with herding sheep.

Our gang (known as the Long Ridge Boys) are Neil Swain, Dougie Swain, Julian Swain, Gary Repetto, Darren Repetto, Paul Repetto, James Glass, Jack Green, Brian Rogers, Mark Swain and myself. Neil who was the local shepherd at that time, has been around to all our houses waking everyone, calling, "It's a day on to the hill."

We arrive at Gary's house to find everyone there except Neil and Dougie who have already left after rousing us out of bed. They almost always pull this trick, just to have the right to announce that they were the first to reach The Base. There is still quite a bit of chill in the air as we set off down to The Bluff, three miles west of the village; amid the barking of the dogs excited at the prospect of going to get sheep. There are a few shouts to be quiet and "Get out of the way" as we leave the village behind, trying to bring the dogs to order.

As we pass Hottentot Gulch, I look up to see several bobbing lights halfway up the mountain, at the back of the village near Goat Ridge. "That's probably Lewis's gang going up for their sheep," I shout to Brian above the noise of the bike's engine. Lewis Glass breeds sheep on the mountain with ten other men. They have been the first team to do so successfully since 1963.

Ten minutes later, having passed The Patches, we park the bikes at the Spring Gulch and walk the last few hundred yards to the foot of the mountain at Burnt Wood. Once there, everyone takes off their sweatshirts and jumpers, stripping to their T-shirts before beginning the ascent of the steep gradient. This is between an angle of 75 to 80 degrees and 833 metres or so to the first base. The mountain then slopes more gently up to the peak (highest point) of the island, about 45 degrees.

01.30: we take out our torches, which we will use on the first section of the climb. We walk in silence, single file, until we are above the Red Sand, an area at the bottom of the mountain caused by erosion which is the size of a football pitch. We have a short rest, pass around some sweets, then set off again, each person walking to their own pace or with another person. Brian and Jack (being the oldest of the group) bring up the rear. Mark, James and myself walk a little ahead of the others, as we prefer to keep going at a steadier pace, not stopping even for short rests. Below us we can hear Brian taking the mickey out of Paul and Darren for having a hangover, after enjoying themselves at the pub the previous night.

A glance at my watch shows it's 02.20: we have all reached the first base to find Dougie and Neil settled comfortably at the main resting place amongst the 'Bog Ferns'. These ferns grow about a metre high and with a trunk as thick as a man's thigh. On top of the base the ground is very marshy with a lot of moss growing on the main path we have to walk on.

Dougie and Neil are looking very chuffed with themselves, having reached the base first ."What's been keeping you'll?" they ask. They get remarks back like, "We got held up by the traffic," or "The train was running late". Brian says he's sure they have been having a sleep whilst waiting for us. Amid the banter we have a sandwich, because once we start herding the sheep, there won't be time to stop for anything until the sheep are penned. "Time to move," says Neil, standing up and shouldering his bag, "It's ten to three already." We set off again walking in single file along a crude path that is very wet, our feet sinking into the marshy ground. Sometimes you walk into a soft bit of ground and end up sinking into the boggy path almost up to the knees.

To get to the sheep, we have to walk three miles in single file along a narrow winding path. Crossing three gulches (ravines) ranging from about 15 to 20 metres in depth, also crossing several smaller gutters about the size of a drainage ditch. This path was made above the wooded area of the base; the trees growing there are very bushy and grow much along the ground, more like a hedgerow. This is caused by the strong winds blowing across the island. The islanders used to cut these trees down in the past to use for firewood. They grow about two metres high and are named *Phylica Arborea* but are known locally as the Island Wood Tree.

04.00: It's starting to get daylight, the black giving way to a pale bluish grey. Neil, Gary. Mark, Julian, James and Jack and I turn off the path and walk inland, upwards, on the rising ground towards the Peak. The others carry on further along the path to Long Ridge to sort out the sheep pen. We walk in silence now following the contours of a ridge keeping just below the skyline.

If the sheep see or hear us they will be away before even the dogs can get to them, but for the time being, the dogs are kept to heel. The sloping ground on which we have had to walk since turning off the path is similar to the landscape of the Brecon Beacons in Wales, or to the Lake District. Our destination is a huge sheer wall of rock with several precipices along the top about 150 metres long and about 30 metres high. This rock formation is known locally as The Castle at Flat Gulch. It certainly looks like a medieval fortress, very majestic, grey and daunting in the pale morning light. The moon still casts deep shadows around the base of the rock formation despite the growing daylight.

We reach the top of the ridge above The Castle and peer over the top. Below us, grazing on a flat area of grass is our flock of sheep. We count up to 50 ewes, most of them have two lambs, several are black. The area in which they are grazing is about the size of a football pitch, but circular, rather like an amphitheatre. The sides are flanked by a ridge of volcanic shingle that starts each side of the 'Castle' and meet together on a narrow saddle shaped ridge of more volcanic shingle, that rises up to the Peak. This was once the crater of a small volcano.

We stop for a few moments off to one side of the ridge, talking in low whispers so as not to alert the sheep. Looking out over The Base to the sea beyond, we can see the sunlight reflecting off the sea, between Nightingale and Inaccessible Islands. To the east, more in the centre of Tristan, there is a much darker patch of water, almost as if there is a shallower section of the seabed. The darker water is wider, close to Tristan but growing narrower to a point where it ends on the horizon. It's the same shape as an ice cream cone - the narrow tip on the horizon, the top against the island, Tristan being the ice cream. We contemplate for a while what could have caused this change in sea colour, as the sun comes over the peak of the island. Mark has the answer: we are looking at the shadow of Tristan being cast out across the water of the Atlantic, a most amazing sight to behold.

By now the sheep have sensed our presence and start to move towards the opposite ridge, but too late, Neil and Gary release their dogs to keep the flock from fleeing. We follow suit with our dogs, flanking each side of the sheep as we drive them down the ridge to the pen below. We are soon down at the pen. There's much shouting of "Look out, that lamb is trying to bust past," ('bust' being Tristan slang for 'get away') as the sheep make frantic efforts to break out of the flock. Slowly the sheep are being forced into the pen. Suddenly, Darren shouts out: "Look out, Big Horns is getting away."

Big Horns is the name of our ram, the leader of the flock. He has an impressive set of horns and is crusty by nature. Brian, who had just opened the gate to the pen, looks up to see the ram rushing at him, his head lowered to butt him. Brian firmly stands his ground. The rest of us look spellbound by the turn of events. The ram is within spitting distance of Brian, when he releases his dog Mac, who, in the twinkling of an eye, brings the ram to ground with a resounding thud. "Thought you would get away," Brian shouts, as he pounces on the ram to hold him down. With the help of Paul, Brian drags the ram into the pen, amidst shouts of laughter from the rest of us. Big Horns joined the rest of the flock, looking very indignant at being thrown to the ground so suddenly.

The first task with the sheep in the pen was to earmark the lambs and castrate the male lambs. Jack stood by the gate, notebook in hand, keeping account of which is male and which is female, as the rest of us catch the lambs for Neil and Gary, who was castrating and earmarking them. The lambs are earmarked so if they wander off from the flock, and get with another flock belonging to someone else, we would be able to identify them as ours.

Soon the lambs have been sorted: a total of 48 for this year. We start shearing the wool off the ewes. This takes about one and a half hours using hand shears. The last sheep to be sheared is Big Horns. The ram seems to be looking for revenge for being toppled, but we know better and don't give him the chance. Jack checks that we have 50 ewes to let go for breeding, the wethers (castrated males) from last year and ewes that have lost their lambs, we take out of the pen to slaughter.

The method for killing sheep on Tristan is holding the neck taut, cutting the sheep's throat using a sharp knife with swift stroke, thus breaking the neck at the same time. Although a few of our group are not up to this task, I just accept it as part of the lifestyle I have to live on Tristan. We slaughter one sheep between two men. It will then be cut in half and each man will put half a sheep into his bag to carry back to the village. A full-grown sheep from the mountain after it has been slaughtered and skinned, weighs about 55 kilos or more. Now that the shearing is finished we are busy skinning the sheep and removing the insides, and then cutting the carcass into halves. By the time we complete this it's about midday. We begin a slow steady walk back down the mountain, stopping for rests along the path, especially when we have to climb in and out of the gulches.

14.00: we are back at the base enjoying the view, looking down on The Patches, the people moving around them as tiny dots of reds, blues, and whites in the distance. The last stage of the journey is walking down Burnt Wood, which is done taking much care to avoid falling over and hurting oneself. Finally we are running down the Red Sand on to the grass at The Bluff, where we stop to clear the sand from our shoes and continue to the Spring Gulch, where we'd parked our motorbikes.

Before we get to them, James notices that Paul, who is walking just in front of him, has an apple protruding from the back of his bag. While a few of us divert Paul's attention, James creeps up behind Paul, giggling, penknife in hand, trying to slit the bag to get the apple out.

He suspects Paul as one of the culprits who swiped his bar of chocolate. But Paul cottons on to what's happening: he is alerted by James, who is laughing too much to get the apple from the bag.

On reaching the village we all go to our homes to wash the carcass of the sheep we carried there, ready for butchering the next day. With that finished, it's time to relax in the bath and then to enjoy the delicious meal the ladies have prepared after our long trek up the mountainside.

18.00: we all meet at Gary's house to have a few beers and plan our next trip on the mountain. Each time we come back from a trip up the mountain, one person takes it in turn to invite others for a social drink at their house, so plans can be made for the next trek up the mountain for sheep. We are all at Gary's except Dougie and Neil, who arrive half an hour later. As they walked into the lounge, Brian says, "What's with you two? Got held up in the traffic?" There was a burst of laughter from around the room. I thought 'Yes'. The banter starts again.

SEARCH & RESCUE REPORTS

Search and Rescue operations on Tristan can be unpredictable at the best of times. Most of the incidents happen at sea, although there have been a few rescues on land. One must bear in mind given the remoteness of Tristan, there is a limit to what resources we can draw upon. Rescue from the air is non-existent. But Tristanian men are a versatile breed well used to dealing with improbable situations in a practical way. Here are some of the Search and Rescue ventures that I have organised and led.

YACHT ABANDONED ON TRISTAN

On Saturday 17th October 1987 at about 16.30, Clive Glass was out at The Patches, when he saw two flares sent up from a yacht about 100 metres offshore at The Hardies. Clive left at once to summon help. I was also out at The Patches ear marking some lambs, with Jack and Brian when I saw the flares, but could only see the top of the yacht's broken mast. I set off for home on my motor bike to help the yacht.

Contact by radio was tried, but was unsuccessful. The Government launch was put out to sea and made contact alongside the yacht, which was by now at Boat Harbour. On the way home I saw the launch pull away from the yacht and head for the harbour. The yacht continued to drift toward the beach at Boat Harbour. I could see a couple of people on the beach at Boat Harbour, so went back there, after asking Brian Rogers and Jack Green to inform Sgt. Albert Glass (the policeman at the time) of my intentions to salvage what I could from the yacht if it washed ashore.

We later found the yacht's name was *Brandgans* (*Heag Padesle*). On board was only one man, a German named Siegbert Mowka. He was just about out of food and water with only about half a litre of fresh water left, several packets of soup and two small tins of rice. He said he had been in a bad storm from the south west which had broken his mast about half way off, and had been travelling with a broken mast for about three to four weeks. He was also out of fuel. He was taken aboard the launch which returned to the Settlement.

The yacht was abandoned. It then drifted towards the beach at Boat Harbour bay. Watching all this were Terence Green, Herbert Glass and Clive Glass and when the yacht was quite close to the beach, a rope was washed overboard towards the shore. Herbert waded into the surf and grabbed the rope and with the help of Terence and Clive, beached the yacht and secured the rope fast to a boulder. They started to remove all clothing, sails and other items from the yacht. I arrived soon after, took charge and helped with the unloading. By 19.00 we had managed to remove most of the goods, and the more personal items were brought home and left with Sgt. Glass. I was instructed by Sgt. Glass along with Terence, Herbert and Clive to collect the rest of the items the next day. The shipwrecked sailor was put into one of the government guest houses for the night after being checked out by Dr Paul Helliwell, who was also Acting Administrator in Roger Perry's absence.

On Sunday 18th, accompanied by Dr. Helliwell, Siegbert, Joe Green, Douglas Swain, Andrea Repetto, Terence, Clive and Herbert, I set off for Boat Harbour to collect the items from the yacht. By 11.00 all the items were hoisted up the cliff and put into the Land Rover, where they were brought to the hospital and unloaded.

I noticed that when Siegbert arrived at Sgt Glass's home before we left for Boat Harbour, he was rather taken aback when he saw the sign 'Police' outside the door and exclaimed in a loud voice "Police" with an astonished look on his face. Another two facts that did not add up was that the name on the stern of the yacht had been crudely painted out in black paint and the sea cocks on the bottom of the yacht were left turned on, so the water could come into the boat.

I found the name of the yacht *Brandgans* (*Heag Padesle*) by rubbing wet sand over the painted-over name and the original letters under the paint were pronounced enough for me to read the name. When we asked Siegbert about this, he said was running away from his wife, who was suing him after their divorce, over the sale of their house. He did not have any passport with him on the yacht. After he left the island and Roger Perry returned, we found out our German friend was in fact wanted by Interpol, in connection with drug smuggling. He remained for a while in Cape Town then stole another yacht and sailed to Rio, where passing yachtsmen mentioned they met him. The last news we heard was that he was found dead on the beach in Rio, murdered for crossing the wrong person.

THE MISSING ADMINISTRATOR

On Sunday 24th April 1994, around 20.00, I was at home when Marius De Boer and Matthew Randall (contractors helping to build the harbour) arrived rather concerned because the Administrator at the time, Philip Johnson, had invited them to a barbecue at his home anytime after 18.00 that evening and it was not like him not to be there. They arrived at the Residency at 18.50 and found the barbecue had been partly set up, the back porch light on and the top half of the front door open. They tried the bell and shouted but there was no answer, so they walked up to the doctor's house. Mr. Johnson was not there either and Dr. John Morris said he had not seen him over the weekend.

19.40: they checked at the Residency again this time going inside, looking in all the rooms, no one was there. Matthew and Marius left a note on the back door and came up and spoke to me about the matter. We stayed at my house for 30 minutes as I thought Mr. Johnson had been out for a walk or was visiting at a birthday party or speaking to one of the Heads of Departments concerning the departure of MV *Hekla*. I asked them if they had checked the office, they said "yes" and his Land Rover garage was still locked.

20.40: we checked the Residency again. No one was there, the note still on the back door. We quickly checked with Father Tony Agreiter (the Catholic priest) and at Matthew's and Marius's residence, no one was there either. I checked inside again, the house was empty. I noticed that his coats were hanging in the hallway and only one cream coloured hat was missing and the office and Land Rover keys were on the hallway table. I then decided to check the homes of Lewis Glass (Chief Islander and Special PC), Benny Green, Allan Swain, Lindsay Repetto, who were the Heads of Departments involved with the MV *Hekla*.

At the home of Lewis Glass, I asked him to accompany me, as this now was a matter for the police. We checked the other homes; no one had seen him for the last 48 hours, only Lewis who said he had seen Mr. Johnson walking over the volcano towards Pigbite between 14.00 and 15.00 on Saturday 23rd April. I called on Special PC Clive Glass to help search. Marius quickly checked at the Residency, no one was there.

21.35: I asked Lewis and Clive to check at Pigbite and Marius, Matthew, Melanie Glass (a WPC) and Marie Repetto to check the harbour and beach from the volcano to Hottentot and the west side of Hottentot Gulch as these were known to be Mr. Johnson's favourite walks. Each group was given a walkie-talkie radio, to keep contact with me.

21.45: I went to the Doc's house and left a radio with him informing him of the situation and asked if he could be ready with the Land Rover and equipment if needed. This he quickly arranged. I left for Allan Swain's house and told him of the events. We then collected my Land Rover, checked the Residency again, then headed for Pigbite.

At 23.30, we reached Pigbite. I liaised with Lewis and Clive and searched the entire area as far as Plantation Gulch, unable to cross the beach to get to the beach at Big Point because of the heavy swell crashing against the cliff or able to get down into the Gulch by the other road, as the rope was broken from the top of the Gulch. We shouted but received no answer.

I contacted the other group: they had not found anything. After calling the Doctor on the radio I asked him to check again with Mary Glass, (the Residency Housekeeper) and Cynthia Green (his Secretary) to make another check at the Residency and his Office and Jack to arrange with Benny to keep the lights on. Matthew, Marius, Melanie and Marie checked the reservoir and the back of the volcano.

23.50: back at the Residency, batteries and torches were collected from the supermarket. Allan Swain sorted out four more radios and the search and rescue rope. After speaking to the people who were on the volcano working on Saturday afternoon and with Mary and Gilbert I learned no one had seen the Administrator except on Saturday, when he was going to Pigbite.

Clive went off to ask Jeffrey, Neil, Herbert, Richard, Harold, Ian and many others he saw on the way to help with the search. Lewis went to call on Lindsay Repetto and Joe Green. Some more men turned up offering to help - Ken and Martin Green, Jack, Larry, Keith, Ronald, Gilbert and Albert Green. Not knowing where to start the search, most people had seen or heard of Mr. Johnson going to Pigbite. It was Lindsay who confirmed what was in the back of most peoples' minds: Mr Johnson had asked several days before if he could get to the rookery by way of the beach past Big Point, to collect different kinds of rock samples.

00.30: I arranged for the men to split into teams, each team with a radio, while I stayed at the Residency with another radio to co-ordinate the search:

Team A: Trevor, Harold, Martin, Larry and Keith to check the beach from the volcano to Hottentot, Bugsby Hole and Hill Piece.

Team B: Joe Green, Ken Green, Allan Swain, Jack, Duncan and Jeffrey left in the Land Rover to check The Bluff back towards Patches at The Farm.

Team C: Herbert Glass, Clive, Richard, Alfred, Neil and Lindsay Repetto took the rope with them to check Pigbite across to Big Point.

Team D: Lewis, Ian, Jeremy and Albert Green checked the area on top of the volcano.

Herbert and Neil set off ahead to check under Big Point as Herbert who had lots of experience of the areas east of Pigbite, knew a path they could get down to the beach without using a rope. Back at the Residency the Doctor and I waited in silence almost willing a message on the radio.

00.45: team A radioed they had covered the Hill Piece to Hottentot Gulch, nothing was found, going to check the beach areas.

00.50: team C radioed that Clive, Alfred, Lindsay and Richard were putting down a rope to get to the beach. Herbert and Neil had started towards Big Point.

00.54: Matthew, Marius, Melanie and Marie arrived at the Residency having checked the back of the volcano finding nothing. I tried to radio team B out West but could make no contact.

01.00: Neil called urgently on the radio from under Big Point, from the sound of his voice I knew something had happened. Herbert's dog had found Mr. Johnson. He was lying in the shelter of a rock and his leg had been badly hurt.

The doctor, Nurse Caryn and I set off for Pigbite by Land Rover. On the way I spoke to Ian and asked if team D could meet us at Pigbite to help with the Doctor's equipment.

01.40: we reached Mr Johnson and team C under Big Point, having climbed down the rope to the beach. Mr Johnson was rather dazed and seemed to be suffering from hypothermia. He had cut the inside of his right leg just above the knee. The Doctor and Caryn quickly made Mr. Johnson comfortable and under the Doctor's directions we strapped Mr Johnson onto the stretcher and began the tedious journey back, clambering over huge boulders on the beach and in the Gulch, and up a steep incline to the top of the Gulch. Having made contact with Allan via Robin on radio, I asked for a few more men to help. Larry, Duncan, Allan and Jeffrey climbed down the rope to help us to the top of the Gulch; they were a dozen more willing hands to help lift Mr. Johnson up on to the top of the Gulch by way of the path that Herbert knew.

03.15: we reached the Land Rover and set off for the hospital.

I radioed Andy back at the village and asked him if he could ask the nurses Frances and Teresa to be ready at the hospital. We arrived at the hospital at 03.40 where I thanked everyone who had helped with the search. They went home as the medical staff took over.

At 05.40, I was able to have a short chat with Mr. Johnson who was looking much better and stronger and no longer in a daze. He could not remember why he went to Pigbite or what caused his accident. At 05.45, I left the hospital for home.

The next day Lindsay sent Herbert Glass with a few men to look for Mr. Johnson's spectacles and a small bag. After searching, they found the glasses in two bits at the bottom of the cliff, on the west bottom point of Plantation Gulch where we deduced he had fallen from a height of 52 feet amongst some boulders. Then, it seemed that suffering from concussion, he had wandered to the spot under the Big Point, where he was found.

LOSS OF POWERBOAT

On Tuesday 4th February 1997 at 09.30, Brandon Dalley, the Administrator, informed me that the fishing vessel MFV *Edinburgh* had lost one of her powerboats (a small fishing boat), while they were fishing at Nightingale Island. The boat had been missing from that day, and there had been a search carried out by the other powerboats, on the North, West and East side of Nightingale, but so far nothing had been found. The weather on the south side of Nightingale was quite rough, thus preventing a detailed search from being carried out.

The MFV *Edinburgh,* and MFV *Kelso,* which were fishing at Inaccessible Island, searched from half a mile to 10 miles offshore. The wind was south-west about 15 to 20 knots with a two-metre swell. The current was running into the north, and it was rather a misty day. It was decided that we would go across in the Fisheries Patrol Boat *Wave Dancer 2* to help with the search from the land, checking the beaches on the south of Nightingale.

We left the harbour at 10.45 into the mouth of a west-north west gale, encountering five metres breaking waves. *Wave Dancer 2* rode the seas well, despite being bounced about like a cork. I got sick and spent the trip in company with a plastic bucket, much to the amusement of Joe Green, Trevor Glass, Terry Green, and Andy Repetto, the crew of the *Wave Dancer 2.* Brendon was more sympathetic, although he probably was amused at the idea of a Tristanian male getting seasick.

We arrived at the main landing rock at Nightingale at 13.30 to find the MFV *Edinburgh* and MFV *Kelso* anchored in the calm waters of the lee. We contacted the MFV *Edinburgh* by radio and they sent one of the powerboats to collect Brendon, Terry and myself to land on Nightingale. Harold Green, a Tristanian who was working on the MFV *Edinburgh* as Fishing Advisor came along to take part in the search. Harold had conducted the inshore search by powerboats the previous day. This made the search area much smaller as Harold is a very experienced fisherman at Nightingale and knows the island very well also.

By 14.00, Brendon, Harold, Terry and I were ashore and conducted a search of the West Side landing area. We had to wait until 15.00

hours whilst Joe made contact via VHF to let us know that the mist had cleared away from the top of the hill on Nightingale Island, thus enabling us to continue with the search on the south side of the island. We set off immediately to walk the three and a half miles across the island having to fight our way the last half of the journey through two-metre high tussock grass, but thanks to Harold, we followed a natural draining ditch and it made walking a lot easier.

15.15: we arrived at the cliff top of Ned's Cave at the South side of Nightingale. While Terry and I took one edge of the cliff and checked the beach, Brendon and Harold checked the other side. We had a clear unobstructed view of the beach below from the top of the cliffs, which has a sheer face about 40 metres high. Although we used a loud hailer to call down to the beach, nothing was seen or heard. The only answers were the barking of a 100 or more fur seals on the beach which were disturbed by our shouting.

18.30: we arrived back at the main landing area, having trekked through the tussock grass again. Having contacted the MFV *Edinburgh* and *Wave Dancer 2* with the result of our search, Joe decided, given weather conditions, they would stay the night at Nightingale and return to Tristan the next day. We stayed ashore at Nightingale for the evening as the *Wave Dancer 2* had only four berths for sleeping. Harold cooked our evening meal of potatoes and petrels (shearwater), which we all enjoyed, including Brendon, who was the last Administrator to have stopped overnight on Nightingale in the last 20 years. At 07.30 the next day with the wind south-west, force 25 knots and sea state force 4, we left Nightingale and arrived back at Tristan at 08.45 hours.

Tuesday 11th February was a fishing day with calm seas. Neil Swain and I went across to Nightingale in the RIB *Tornado* (*Wave Dancer 1*) to make a final inspection of the beaches from the south side. Greg Pontichelli (Factory Manager), James Glass and Mike Batty (Fisheries Officer) followed in *Wave Dancer 2* carrying a small rubber zodiac, which we towed behind the RIB around Nightingale and landed on all the beaches to look for any evidence of the lost powerboat, but nothing was found. We returned to Tristan at 16.30 hours.

To finish off the search for the missing powerboat, Brendon, Joe and I carried out a further search of the beaches around Tristan on

Wednesday 12th February 1997, using the RIB *Wave Dancer 1* after it was reported that something that looked like an oilskin jacket was spotted on the beach at Jew's Point. As it was a fishing day, the weather was nice, so after stopping off at The Caves we circumnavigated Tristan, but did not find any wreckage from the lost boat.

Of the boat and the two lost fishermen, nothing was ever found, but a memorial stone is erected in the cemetery on Tristan. It reads:

***M.F.V.* Edinburgh**
In loving memory of Malami Joseph Mbanya and
Gladstone Vuyane Nono
Lost at sea 3rd February 1997
Rest In Peace.

RESCUE ATTEMPT ON GOUGH ISLAND: NOVEMBER 2000

(Edited extracts from my police notes of the incident)

On Friday 17th November 2000, I was informed by the Acting Administrator, James Glass, that the Captain of MFV *Edinburgh* had reported that one of the ship's small fishing boats had capsized and sunk in Battle Bay at Gough Island, 220 miles from the main Tristan island.

One of the boat's crew managed to get ashore on to a small beach; the other person had been picked up by another boat, and brought back to the MFV *Edinburgh*. Although efforts were made to revive him, he was found to be dead when they reached the ship. Battle Bay is situated on the north-west side of Gough. With the wind blowing from that direction, about force 2 to 3 with a one and a half to two metre swell, it was impossible to rescue the man from the beach by boat.

Sunday 19th November at 17.00, I was summoned to the Administrator's office, and told that three further rescue attempts had failed, the last one ending in disaster. The MFV *Edinburgh*'s RIB had been caught in the surf and overturned; leaving another man dead, and two more stranded on the beach with the first man. The three of them had retrieved the body of the dead seaman, when it washed ashore on to the beach.

I was asked to organise some Tristan men to take part in rescue operations at Gough or get some supplies to the men on the beach until a concrete rescue plan could be formulated. We took the police inshore rescue boat, a RIB Tornado 5.3 metres long, with a central steering consul, powered by 40 hp Mariner Outboard. We carried a 15 hp Mariner as a backup motor. We also took a 2 metre rubber inflatable, belonging to the Natural Resources Department.

The men I asked to go to Gough were: Neil Swain, my co-coxswain for the RIB, Herbert and Lewis Glass, for their experience in fishing at Gough and walking on the mountains there. James Glass, Acting Administrator, accompanied us, as he also is very experienced about Gough and its waters. The rest of the team consisted of Greg Ponticelli (Factory Manager) and myself.

At 17.30 all parties were informed that we would board MFV *Kelso* for the trip to Gough. By 19.30 we were at the harbour with all our equipment; there was a heavy swell breaking through the harbour entrance. Using the Police RIB and factory barge we waited until Joe Green, judging the right set of waves, called us safely through the harbour entrance. The light was fading fast.

The MFV *Kelso* hove to at the anchorage; the factory barge made a quick about turn after unloading our gear and scooted back into the harbour, before it got dark. Then it was our turn to get hoisted on board. When at 20.08 the Police RIB was secured, the MFV *Kelso* sailed for Gough Island. Monday 20th November: the MFV *Kelso* arrived at Battle Bay, Gough Island, approximately 13.15. There was north-west wind blowing force 2 with a two-metre swell topped by a very confused sea. We hove to about 1,000 metres off-shore, roughly midway between Isolda and Tristania rocks. The MFV *Edinburgh* was also anchored at Battle Bay.

We could see the men on the beach. Checking the area through binoculars we saw that there seemed to be a heavy surf breaking on the beach, Greg spoke to the Captain of the MFV *Edinburgh*, then to the men on the beach by VHF radio. One had an injury to his ankle and one had a back injury, the other could not hear without his hearing aid.

We explained to them the plan of action that we had formulated: Neil, James, Greg, and I would use the Police RIB. Then, we planned to get in as close as we thought possible; fire a rocket line ashore, to which a 10 mm rope would be attached. The rubber zodiac would then be tied to the rope; the prevailing end would be secured to one of the MFV *Kelso*'s power boats, crewed by Herbert and Lewis 50 metres offshore from the Police RIB. All the men needed to do, was to pull the line with the rubber boat attached on to the beach, collect the body of the dead man, hold the rubber boat at the water's edge, and wait for the right set of waves, then climb into the boat. The powerboat crewed by Herbert

Lewis would tow them to safety, where we could then transferred them to the RIB.

The men on the beach did not seem too keen on the idea and said that there were quite large swells breaking on the beach and large jagged rocks in the water's edge. Greg volunteered to be pulled ashore in the rubber boat, wearing his wet suit if the sea conditions were suitable, to help the people on the beach, because they did not appear to be very optimistic. James, Neil and I decided to launch the RIB so we could get in closer to assess the situation. By this time, the tide was at its lowest ebb and the wind had started to increase. The MFV *Kelso* moved back to the calmer waters of Lot's Wife Cove, where we launched the RIB

Immediately we did so, we started to encounter a very confused sea, which grew worse as we turned into Battle Bay. Neil kept an eye out for any freak waves, while James pointed out the reefs to me. From my point of view, I was sailing into uncharted waters. On James' instruction, we stopped about 450 metres from the shore; the surf line started about 300 metres out. It would have been dangerous to go any closer because there were a number of fishing buoys, forming a line about 50 metres in front of us, the entire length of the bay. These belonged to the powerboat that had sunk; they had a lot of slack line attached to them, so we could not risk getting inside the buoys for fear of fouling the outboard propeller.

Suddenly Neil shouted, "Connie, watch out for that swell on the port side." Looking up I saw a freak wave, four metres high and six metres away about to break on top of the RIB. I spun the wheel hard to port, pushing the throttle fully open. The RIB leapt forward with Neil and James holding on for dear life, as I pointed the bows towards the breaking wave. With the RIB facing the breaking wave, I cut the boat's speed, allowing the wave to pass the RIB'S bow. I increased speed again running over the wake of the wave; the RIB surfing down the trough to safety from the unseen reefs. This skill in boat handling I learned from my father and it's something all Tristan men are capable of doing. Neil radioed the MFV *Kelso* that the weather was too bad for any rescue attempt, and that we were going back to the lee in Transvaal Bay.

A quarter of an hour later, we were back on the ship. Captain Nick told us that two members from the South African meteorological team on Gough, had set off over the mountain to try to get supplies to the men on the beach, but had been forced to turn back to base camp due to bad weather. The ship anchored off the New Weather Station and we went ashore to speak to the team leader on Gough. I told him if we did not get the men off the beach, or get supplies ashore to them by boat, we would try to reach them by walking over the mountain, but would need their assistance for such a venture. The leader offered to help in any way they would could, we stayed ashore for tea, returning to the MFV *Kelso* at 18.00, having spent a pleasant time ashore.

Tuesday 21st November: wind still north west force 3, about a three metre swell running. At 07.30, left Transvaal Bay for Battle Bay, arrived at 08.00 and dropped anchor. The weather was worse than yesterday, with very poor visibility. Spoke to the guys on the beach, they were running short of food, but had a constant supply of drinking water (there is a waterfall running from the mountain onto the beach). They were given instructions on how to survive, collecting driftwood and dry tussock grass to make a fire with; they also had matches and petrol from the RIB that had washed ashore. They were told that they had been granted permission to kill penguins and shearwater petrels and take their eggs if they ran out of food. They replied, "This is a bird sanctuary, we can't kill the birds." So much for survival of the fittest!! Returned to anchor at The Old Glen at 18.00, weather still the same.

Wednesday 22nd November: wind north west, weather much the same as yesterday. 06.00: returned to anchor at Battle Bay, contacted the party on shore. They had finished the last of their food. Again they were told how to catch and cook the birds. Contacted the South African meteorological station on Gough: the leader said that the two-team members had returned safely, and were standing by if needed. Ovenstone Agencies, the South African fishing company which owns both fishing vessels, were informed of the situation, and a plan was implemented to send for a ship with a helicopter to rescue the men from the beach. We could not predict when the sea would be calm enough to rescue them by boat - a mountain rescue was out of the question, because of the terrain and the injuries the men had sustained getting ashore. We would try to get supplies to them down the sheer cliff face, which is about 400 to 500 metres high. But at present, we could only hope to get supplies to them if the weather moderated, if not by boat, then by walking over the mountain with enough food until the rescue ship arrived. At 18.00, with the wind backing to west-north west, the MFV *Kelso* returned to anchor at Long Beach.

Thursday, 23rd November: wind west south west, speed 15 knots: 06.30, MFV *Kelso* set off for Battle Bay, arrived there at 07.15, about two metre swell running and the sea much calmer, the waves more in a set pattern. After holding a brief meeting, we decided to execute our previous plan for getting supplies to the men on the beach. 08.00, the MFV *Kelso* returned to the lee at Cave Cove and we launched two powerboats and the RIB. Herbert and Lewis, with a fisherman from the MFV *Kelso* were in one boat, three men from the MFV *Kelso* were in another boat. James, Neil, Greg, and I were in the Police RIB.

The RIB reached Battle Bay first; while waiting for the others to catch up, I took the RIB in past the buoys to within about 200 metres from the shore. After watching the wave patterns, we decided it would be a safe area to work in. The men on shore and boats and ships were all in contact with each other on VHF radio, Greg instructed the party on shore of our plans.

Soon the other boats arrived; Herbert brought his boat in and passed the 10 mm line, which was then attached to the RIB, so if we got in danger they could tow us to safety. The other boat waited further out to help if needed. I moved back to our original position and Herbert moved his boat about 70 metres offshore from us. Greg got ready to fire the rocket line, while James and Neil tied the end of the line to a coil of 10 mm rope we had with us. Greg fired two rockets. The line broke on both. We radioed the other boat and asked them to go to the MFV *Kelso* and get another rocket gun. The MFV *Kelso* and others were informed of the events. The rocket gun they brought back was a different type than the first two.

Captain Nick gave Greg instructions on its use via VHF; unfortunately, he did not understand them too well, so we returned to the MFV *Kelso*. Greg hopped on board and went over the instructions again with Nick. Soon we were back in position again; this time Greg fired off a perfect shot, while James somehow got his thumb burnt by the friction of the moving line, much to our amusement. Once the men on the beach had the line and started to pull it in, Neil quickly tied our rope to the rope that was attached to the coil that Lewis was holding in the other boat.

When the men on the beach had the 10mm rope, Lewis tied on the four bundles of supplies, which were fastened on to it, about five metres apart and threw them into the water. They were supported by marker buoys to give them extra buoyancy; Lewis retained his end of the rope, which he tied to an anchored marker buoy, once the supplies were ashore. With Greg on the radio, we used the RIB to keep the line straight as it was pulled onto the beach.

10.30: all the supplies were safely ashore. We motored back to The Old Glen where the MFV *Kelso* picked us up. By 11.20, all the boats were hoisted on board. One of the fishermen ashore complained that he had been sent the wrong brand of tobacco and could we send ashore condensed milk as he did not like the cartons of semi-skimmed milk! Captain Nick was livid and told the fishermen ashore what he thought of them, for being so ungrateful.

17.40: Captain Nick, James, and I went aboard the MFV *Edinburgh* to talk to Captain Clarence. He could only confirm what we had already heard about the accidents on the 17th and 19th November. In fact, two of his rockets' lines had misfired, then on the third attempt, his RIB had been caught in the surf and overturned. The full story would not emerge until the inquest that was held in Cape Town. The rockets that failed were made by Pains Wessex of England - and they were not out of date.

I left the 15 hp motor from the police RIB for the MFV *Edinburgh* to use with the MFV *Kelso*'s spare rescue boat, on the understanding that if lost or damaged, Ovenstone Agencies would replace or rectify as needed. 18.30: we returned to the MFV *Kelso* which sailed at 20.00 for Tristan, as a South African Navy ship, the SAS *Protea*, would reach Gough on the 28th November to complete the rescue, using a helicopter. On the way, we received some wonderful news: Herbert's first grandson had been born in Cape Town. Greg produced a bottle of whisky and we celebrated the new addition to the Glass clan.

Friday 24th November: 19.40 - arrived at Tristan, anchored at West Goat Road Gulch, because there was a huge swell at the harbour. Saturday 25th November, 06.30: MFV *Kelso* hauled anchor, set off for the harbour, arrived at 07.00 and dropped anchor. By 07.30, the entire rescue party was safely back at the harbour.

It's my view that the events of the above report which caused two men to lose their lives, and left another three stranded on the beach, should not have happened. It was the result of the coxswain of the lost powerboat not listening to the advice of his Captain, after leaving the ship. This set off a chain of events in which two men lost their lives, largely due to inexperience in boat handling. One of them, Quentin, was a good friend of mine and a good friend to many Tristanians.

POSTSCRIPT: At the inquest, it was proved that the accident could have been prevented if the fishermen and the coxswain of the RIB had had more knowledge of boat handling.

TOURISM AND IMMIGRATION

It is something of an understatement to say that Tristan da Cunha has always been difficult to reach. That was not necessarily unique during the era of the sailing ships. However, even with the advent of steam ships and then, motor driven vessels, it still takes about seven days to reach Tristan from the nearest port, Cape Town, which is 1,743 miles away. Yes, one thousand seven hundred and forty three miles across the South Atlantic Ocean. There's no airport and no means of reaching the island by air: no chance of a 'Channel Tunnel' being built here to spirit us on a high speed train under the ocean to South Africa!

Cruise ships have been calling at Tristan since the early 1920's. The most memorable – in the recollections of older Tristan people - were Cunard's RMS *Coronia* and the RMS *Asturias*, which after war service and rebuilding, ended her days as she was about to be broken up as the film double for the RMS *Titanic* in 1957. Other cruise ships that have called at Tristan are: the *QE2* in the summer of 1999, the MV *Viking Sea* and MV *Viking Sky* in 1982 and 1983, the MV *Astor* in 1994, MV *Rotterdam* in 1982, April 1996 and March 1998. The cruise ships MV *World Discoverer* and MV *Marco Polo* also called in the nineties. Some of these have been recognised with issues of Tristan's famous postage stamps.

These ships did not land any passengers on Tristan. The first cruise ship to land its passengers was the MV *Lindblad Explorer* on 25th December 1975 – yes, Christmas Day. The weather was perfect. During the day, the ship's crew in their rubber zodiacs landed the passengers. There were about 60 passengers in all, each of the passengers in ones or twos were invited to join the island families for Christmas lunch, the Tristanian way. Once ashore, they were introduced to their hosts, who showed them complete Tristan hospitality for the day. I remember being only 16 years old, walking through the village, greeted by numerous passengers calling "Merry Christmas" to every Tristanian they met. The next day the ship was going to call at Nightingale, but had to abandon the plan because the weather had blown up into a full north-east gale.

The MV *Lindblad* was to visit Tristan again later in the nineties, but renamed MV *Explorer*. The first cruise ship to land passengers on Nightingale was the MV *Explorer*. On Saturday 18th March 1995 there were about 65 passengers in all. We landed the passengers at the west side of Nightingale with a north-west wind and calm seas. The guides were James Glass, Neil Swain, Jeffery Rogers, Alan Swain, Ronald Rogers, Stanley Swain, and myself. The MV *Explorer* was the first also to have their passengers hike to the base at Burntwood, a party of 16 accompanied, by Neil Swain and Ronald Rogers as guides. (The MV *Explorer* subsequently sank after hitting an iceberg off King George Island, 1,700 miles south of Cape Horn).

The MV *Hanseatic* tried to land passengers on Nightingale on Sunday 5th March 1995, but although the weather was quite nice, there was a heavy ground swell at the island, which prevented passengers from landing.

The next vessels to land passengers on Nightingale were the Russian converted oceanographic survey ships, MV *Professor Molchanov* and MV *Professor Khromov* (later renamed MV *Spirit of Enderby*) who landed 36 passengers between them on 23rd March 1995.

When I arrived back from Police Training in the UK in September 1993, I took over the Search and Rescue role along with Customs and Immigration and Conservation duties. With the arrival of the cruise ships in the nineties, Brendon Dalley, the Administrator at the time, appointed me Liaison Officer for all visiting cruise ships, as I was involved with the other aspects of search and rescue, immigration, and conservation. Brendon then picked a list of guides from the Government staff. I would be in charge of organising the guides for the visits of cruise ships. The list consisted of myself, and James Glass as Conservation Officers, Stanley Swain as Harbour Master, Allan Swain and Ronald Rogers, Karl Hagan (who now works for the factory), Neil Swain, Jeffrey Rogers, Jack Green, Richard Green, (and Harold Green and Herbert Glass who are now retired).

The next Administrator, Brian Baldwin, included a few more guides: Warren Glass who works for Fisheries Department and my son, Leon Glass, who helped at the time with the *Tristan Times* on-line newspaper, taking photos and collecting information on cruise ships. The latest guide is Robin Repetto, who was picked by Bill Dickson, a subsequent Administrator. Lewis Glass is also on the list of guides because he is a special police constable. Lewis has retired from the police.

During my absence, Neil Swain takes charge of the guides, as he is my executive officer in charge of search and rescue. If any of the guides are absent, then Mark Swain and Duncan Lavarello, who are coxswains for the search and rescue RIB will fill in for them.

On our first visit to Nightingale with the passengers, one of them asked me why the penguins ran off to the tussock when they are approached. "Madam," I solemnly told her, "the penguins have just received a culture shock and are not used to having their photographs taken by dozens of people with cameras. They are rather shy at having their photograph taken without their make-up on." She walked away to explain this to some of her friends, much to the amusement of one of the ship's staff!

When first boarding cruise ships to clear them for immigration, a number of passengers are surprised to find us dressed in the uniforms of British police officers. I sometimes get the impression that they rather expect us to be wearing grass skirts, covered in face paint with a bone through our nose. While having breakfast on board a recent cruise ship, MV *Endeavour*, one of its American passengers approached our table and exclaimed: "Why, you look just like us!"

I looked up at him rather disdainfully and replied, "What did you hope to find Sir, the missing link?" He walked away rather embarrassed by my reply.

During the visit of the MV *Professor Molchanov*, on Saturday 4th April 1998, the weather was quite nice. The passengers landed and walked about the village, and visited the Craft Shop and Post Office. I organised guides to take some hikers up to the base of Burntwood. All went as planned. The next day we went across to Nightingale, although the sky was overcast, the sea was quite calm. The guides for that trip were myself, Harold, Jack, Jeffrey, Richard Karl, Herbert and Neil.

The MV *Professor Molchanov* arrived at Nightingale at 09.00. The passengers landed at the west side landing, again all went well, Herbert and Neil setting off with the first group of 12 to show them the first pond. Jack and Harold followed with the next group, while Karl and Jeff followed with the rest. Richard and I followed with a few of the less active passengers.

During this time, I noticed an Asian-looking man of about five feet, five inches tall and of slight built. I saw he was having some difficulty when he walked up a slope, but refused the help of any of the ship's staff or guides. I was later to learn that his name was Mr. Patel. He was British by birth and very independent by nature. When Richard and I caught up with him I asked him if he needed any help, he said no, he was alright. He walked with our group until we reached the tussock grass, where they spent an hour or so taking photos of the wildlife. Leaving Richard with the group, I set off to check on the other passengers and guides that were taking photos of penguins down on the main landing rock.

I returned almost an hour later and noticed that Mr. Patel was missing from the group. When I asked Richard, he said he told him he was going down the path a little way to take some photos and he had only been gone about ten minutes or so. I told Richard that I would go to see where he was. I set off down the path to the west side with a feeling all was not well. I quickly covered the distance to the west landing, and descended the path that leads from the cliff to the landing rock. Mr. Patel was nowhere in sight. The feeling of unease got worse. As I turned the last bend on the path before it reaches the rocks, I saw Mr. Patel sitting in the middle. As I reached him I knew something was wrong. He was rather pale in the face and was shivering as in shock.

"Are you alright, Mr. Patel?" I asked.

"No," he replied. "I think I have broken my hip!"

I noticed that his left leg was buried in the soil up past his ankle. "Do you feel any pain?" I asked, examining his right thigh.

"No," he replied, "but I have a steel pin in my right hip, due to an accident. While riding a bicycle, I got hit by a bus in London. I tried to get up but my right leg feels numb and awkward to move."

"Don't move," I said. "It will only make things worse. I'll get help."

I called the ship but did not receive any answer. I called the other guides on their VHF radios, Richard answered. I told him what had happened and asked him to relay the message to the others, and asked them if they could come down to the west side and bring the passengers with them, as I would need their help.

Then I got a call from the expedition leader, Rinie van Meurs. I told him what had happened. He radioed the ship and called the doctor and for a stretcher. Within a few minutes Rinie, Richard, Jeff and Karl had reached us. Harold and Jack came with the rest of the passengers, with Herbert and Neil bringing up the rear.

Mr. Patel told us the ground gave way under his foot and that had caused him to fall. On closer inspection, I saw that he had stepped on top of a shearwater's burrow, the top had caved in and that had caused the fall. Over a million shearwaters are estimated to nest on Nightingale and build their nests underground. This makes walking there quite dangerous.

Soon the doctor arrived from the ship with several of the crew. The doctor and crew were Russian and did not speak very good English - indeed, virtually none. After examining Mr. Patel, the doctor instructed the crew to put Mr. Patel onto the stretcher. Trying to be as careful as possible with him, the Russian crew lifted him onto the stretcher, but when he cried out in pain and told them to stop, they could not understand him. Rinie had to stop them, liaise with the doctor and back to Mr. Patel, then to the crew. By this time Mr. Patel was screaming blue murder at the crew: it was just as well they did not understand him!

As they strapped Mr. Patel onto the stretcher, the doctor suddenly spoke to him in Russian, then diving into his bag, he produced a syringe and said to us: "injection". He stopped the crew from moving the stretcher, and injected Mr. Patel, then spoke to Rinie, who told us the doctor said that he could not be moved for twenty minutes until the injection had taken full effect. Mr. Patel groaned and said: "That bloody doctor, the only words in English he speaks are pain and injection".

While we were waiting, I told Rinie that it would be best if we started to boat the other passengers back to the ship. He agreed, and the Russian crew with the help of Neil, Jack and Jeff started taking the other passengers back to the MV *Professor Molchanov*. By the time 20 minutes had passed, only a few passengers were left so I told Rinie I thought it would be better if he let the guides take Mr. Patel on the stretcher to the boat and onto the ship. He understood us alright, and as we were used to handling boats by the rock and on the side of the ship. He agreed, and everything went smoothly, even moving the stretcher through the narrow passages on the ship to the hospital cabin.

When moving Mr. Patel, I kept explaining each move we were going to make with the stretcher, so he knew what to expect on the journey to the ship. Once everyone was back on board we sailed for Tristan, trying to make contact with Tristan Radio. After an hour we raised them. I then spoke to Dr Wendy and told the Administrator what had happened. Dr Wendy prepared the hospital for our arrival. It was dark when we reached Tristan. I came ashore in a zodiac to pick up Dr Wendy and the Administrator, and on the way back to the ship gave them the story again in more detail.

Once on board, Dr Wendy took charge and after examining Mr. Patel said that he would have to go ashore. She would need to deal with him at the hospital. Rinie said the ship would stay until Mr. Patel was well enough to travel. At eight o'clock the guides, the Administrator, Mr. Patel and the Russian doctor came ashore. The guides assisted Dr Wendy with Mr. Patel to the hospital where our nurses had the x-ray machine ready. The Administrator thanked the guides and told them to take the next day off work, having conducted themselves so professionally.

Dr Wendy asked me to stay at the hospital to help. The nurses took the X-rays of Mr. Patel's hip. Rinie and I would turn him with Dr Wendy's guidance. Once that was finished, we helped Dr Wendy and the nurses pull Mr. Patel's leg as Dr Wendy set the hip into place. Then she covered it with plaster of Paris. Mr. Patel was admitted to one of the hospital wards for the night. During this time, the Russian doctor stood to one side, as he could not understand enough English to follow Dr Wendy's instructions. He was most relieved when Rinie explained to him all was well. At 23.15, Rinie and the doctor went back to the ship.

Next morning at 09.30, the weather was still nice. I went to the hospital to speak to Dr Wendy. Mr. Patel was looking much better. Dr

Wendy was rather concerned about Mr. Patel travelling on the ship with the Russian doctor not being able to speak hardly any English. I told her that there were two retired English nurses among the passengers. I had already met them and was rather surprised that they lived near Bristol, where my wife Sharon's aunt and uncle live. We had already swapped addresses, and had planned to meet up in Bristol when Sharon and I visited there to spend Christmas with Leon, who was studying at Denstone College in Staffordshire at that time.

Dr Wendy made contact with the ship, spoke to Rinie, and they came ashore and spoke to her and agreed with the consent of the Russian doctor and Rinie that they would help to take care of Mr. Patel until the MV *Professor Molchanov* reached Ascension Island, where he would be flown home to the UK. With everything sorted, Mr. Patel was taken back on board the MV *Professor Molchanov* and she sailed for Ascension Island. A few months later, we heard from Mr. Patel. He had made a complete recovery and sent his special thanks to Dr Wendy for setting his hip in place.

People from any ship that calls at Tristan often ask if there is much policing to do, seeing that Edinburgh-of-the-Seven-Seas is such a quiet village. Well, my answer to them is that I am responsible for more than policing the island. My other jobs are immigration, conservation, helping the fisheries department, search and rescue, maintenance of the rescue RIB, visits liaison officer and agent for visiting cruise ships, sorting out the arrangements for their itinerary, taking charge of guides for cruise ships and welfare officer. They are amazed that on Tristan we have to carry out so many jobs!

VISITING CRUISE SHIPS: NOT ALWAYS PLAIN SAILING

Those interested in visiting Tristan, its shipping and transport and travel, will be interested to look at a recent year's traffic in cruise ships. So we'll look at the five which called at Tristan in 2003, beginning in January and finishing in April. As the story relates, reaching the most remote inhabited island in the world, even from the comfort, safety and luxury of a cruise ship, is often far from easy – and sometimes impossible.

A lot of work is involved in making the itinerary arrangements for the arrival of each ship, but however carefully we may plan for the visits, it's the weather which directs what action is taken. For on Tristan, the weather reigns supreme. It dictates whether it's a day for fishing, offloading the cargo, going to Nightingale or re-roofing a house or working at The Patches.

The weather played a part in the unfortunate bad luck with some of the cruise ships. The first was on the 21st January with the arrival of the RMS *St Helena*. Whilst disembarking the official party, there was quite a heavy swell at the gangway and one of the ship's crew got his legs crushed between the boat and the ship, and had to be admitted to hospital.

The arrival of the MV *Astoria* with 500 passengers on board was on 16th February. The swell prevented the Captain from letting his passengers land; he said it was too dangerous to let them get from the ship into the boat. However, we did manage to put the Handicraft and Post Office personnel on board with Immigration using the small rescue RIB, but the passengers did not have their passports stamped, so we did not make any money on immigration fees.

The third incident was a bit of drama with the arrival of the MV *Endeavour* on the 15 March. The MV *Endeavour* personnel have been here before and know the procedure for landing passengers at Tristan. To begin with, there were some mean sets of swells running through the harbour just over a meter high but, nothing that could not be handled if the zodiac drivers listened to the Harbour Master (Stanley Swain) giving instructions when he was calling time. The zodiacs are powered by 50 hp Honda, four- stroke outboards and should have had more than enough power to run between the waves to get into the harbour. After the ship dropped anchor, the boat arrived to pick up the immigration team with the cruise director in it. Stanley and I explained about the swell at the harbour and suggested that we would clear the ship for immigration, while we waited for the tide to get high, by then it would be safer to disembark passengers.

We boarded the ship and stamped passports, also to check that all the indemnity forms were also signed. While we were stamping passports, the cruise director asked if it would be alright to start landing passengers. He said they had sent another scout boat to check out conditions at the harbour and did not see any problem with landing passengers. I told him it was fine by me but I would like to go ashore in the first boat to make arrangements with the guides. I left Lorraine and Lewis stamping passports and went ashore to organise the guides for hikers going up the volcano.

On the way in, the boat in which I was traveling in seemed to have engine problems and I had to prime the fuel line, as we ran through the harbour, so the outboard would not stop. There did not seem to be much speed on the engines. Usually, these engines have enough power to outrun any swell coming in the harbour. Stanley also noticed this and we inquired what the problem was, and was told it was a fuel problem and they would fix it.

Several boatloads of passengers later, a couple of boats seemed to be having similar problems with their engines. Again, Stanley told the Cruise Director that he was not happy about the turn of speed the boats were showing coming into the harbour. We were told that the engines were old and it was alright to continue landing the passengers. Taking no chances from our side, we uncoiled the life ring on the harbour just in case. As luck would have it, one boat carrying six passengers was caught by a swell about one metre high just as the boat reached the inner west point of the harbour. Instead of keeping the boat straight and riding the swell into the harbour, the zodiac driver turned to look over his shoulder at the approaching wave, turning the outboard as he did so, causing the boat to slew to the left and the wave caught it at the same time, resulting in the boat tipping to its starboard side, throwing four passengers into the harbour and then crabbing sideways into the east part of the harbour.

Jeff Rogers and I were on the Inner West point and witnessed this. I have often read how things seem to slow down to people involved in accidents, almost as if one is watching an action scene on television played in slow motion. Well, this happened to me during this incident. Everything seemed much clearer, and in sharper focus. Was this because of an adrenaline rush? I don't know – only that I did not think: I just reacted. I feel it was my police and search and rescue training guiding my actions. Jeff shouted, "What are we going to do?" I told him to throw the life ring with the line attached to the passengers in the water and I shouted to them to grab onto it.

All of them were wearing inflated life jackets; three of them managed to grab on to the life ring, but the fourth was having difficulty with the straps on his life jacket. They were loose, causing it to come tight under his neck, making it difficult for him to breathe. Meanwhile the current was taking him out of the harbour. Telling Jeff to pull the life ring into the side of the harbour, I threw off my police hat, tie, radio and shoes and leapt into the harbour to help him. I remember being rather surprised how quickly and easy it was to swim despite being partly clothed. As soon as I reached the man, I told him to relax and pulled down on the straps of his life jacket, relieving the pressure under his neck.

Suddenly, Loran Bonnardot, a Frenchman visiting some Tristan friends, appeared and with his help, we soon had all the passengers clinging on to the life ring, and with the help of Martin, Gavin, Grant Green, Simon Glass, and John Lavarello, who had just returned from The Caves with Loran, Jeff pulled us into the landing steps and out of the water.

The man I rescued was taken to hospital to be checked out, as he seemed to be in shock. Loran, who is a doctor, accompanied him to

The sign that says it all!
Photo: author's collection

The sun picks out the snowy peak of Tristan's volcanic profile which soars dramatically from the depths of the South Atlantic.
Photo: Chris Bates

Miniature sheet of stamps issued by the Tristan Post Office honouring my direct ancestor, William Glass, founder of the colony and first governor.
Casco Philatelic/Tristan da Cunha Post Office

Gravestone of William Glass, founder and first governor of the colony.
Photo: Brian Rogers

S.A. *Agulhas* off Edinburgh of the Seven Seas, the island capital.
Photo: James Glass

View of Edinburgh of the Seven Seas from the new volcano.
Photo: Brian Rogers

The Potato Patches - me and my family planting spuds.
Photo: Chris Bates

Our new harbour crane, which has replaced the one which collapsed, transforming goods handling – but ships still have to unload at sea onto our pontoon and into small boats, to send freight into the harbour.

Photo: Leon Glass

The new fishing factory nears completion to replace the one burned down. It has been built to EU standards which should enable our crayfish to be sold in Europe.

Photo: Leon Glass

What else could I be but a Rockhopper Copper on patrol in this 'Penguin Police' day-glow jacket? *Photo: David Mackenzie*

My Police Land Rover is essential for access on Tristan's rough terrain.
Photo: David Mackenzie

A rookery of Rockhopper Penguins.
Photo: James Glass

Fur seals on Nightingale Island.
Photo: Richard Grundy

The errant oil rig firmly aground and abandoned off Tristan. It was eventually made environmentally safe and sunk in deeper water.
Photo: Julie Bates

In Vlissingen in The Netherlands, with Sharon in 2009, for the naming of Oceanwide Expeditions' new vessel for their Tristan cruises and Polar voyages, the MV *Plancius*.
Photo: Chris Bates

Me with the other Immigration Officer,
my sister-in-law, Lorraine Repetto.

At work on the cruise liner MS *Hanseatic* with (left to right) the Purser, me, Lorraine and Iris Green who also helped with immigration matters.
Photos: author's collection

The Twitchers have landed!
The first cruise ship passengers ever to come ashore on Inaccessible Island queue to see its unique Flightless Rail.

Nightingale Island: cruise ship passengers up close and personal with a Yellow Nosed Albatross.

Photos: author's collection

My son Leon celebrating his 21st birthday by helping to land cruise passengers on Inaccessible Island.

Close contact sailing – my boat *Raffee* in a summer race.
The skill lies in taking the wind out of your competitors' sails!
James Glass

The sea's ferocious surges constantly damage our harbour breakwaters, making further repairs necessary in 2011 to enable us to survive as a community. *Photo: Leon Glass*

The *Canton*.
Richard Grundy

On Nightingale Island, the long boat *Britannia* being manhandled ashore on the landing rock showing the strenuous technique involved.
Photos: author's collection

A last – and the most remote – outpost of what was once the British Empire: The Residency, home today of Her Majesty's Administrator of Tristan da Cunha.
Photo: Chris Bates

Repairs under way on the harbour: despite the Sappers' best efforts, not entirely successful in the face of merciless battering from South Atlantic storms, necessitating a further £6 million pounds expenditure in 2011.
Photo: Leon Glass

My parents Monica and Edwin (Spike) Glass with one of the last bullock carts in use on the island in 1984. The animals are Nep (on the left) and my bullock Sandy: taken on the way to The Patches.
Richard Grundy

Inaccessible Island from Tristan.
Brian Rogers

My son Leon and me with Chris Bates (right) during his visit to the island in 2006. Chris is now the UK Representative of the Tristan da Cunha Government. *Photo: Julie Bates*

Where today's Tristan community started - Floors Castle, home of the Dukes of Roxburghe in Kelso in the Scottish Borders, where my 7xgreat-grandfather William Glass worked, before joining the British Army and his fateful posting to Tristan. I found it an extraordinary experience while in Kelso (to plan a Tristan Film Festival) to walk the streets and use the buildings he had known. *Photo: Chris Bates*

the hospital. The others seemed alright and were given blankets to keep them warm. Stanley, seeing this, closed the harbour to further use of the boats. After a brief discussion with the ship's staff, no more passengers were landed and the immigration team was still on the ship. The 36 passengers who were already ashore were taken off later when the tide was high at 11.30 and Lewis and Lorraine came ashore. The passenger at the hospital didn't need any medical attention and went back to the ship with the others.

Although attempts were made at landing passengers the following day, this had to be aborted as there was too much swell. The MV *Endeavour* departed without landing all of its passengers.

The MV *Professor Molchanov* was the last cruise ship of the year to call, managing to land passengers at Tristan, Nightingale and Inaccessible. It's the first time we had allowed people to land at Inaccessible. This was done as a trial run after much deliberation between James and myself. The 51 passengers and staff were landed along with the eight local guides. The passengers saw the flightless rail, a small bird that cannot fly and is only found on Inaccessible, they also saw an elephant seal and some baby fur seals.

CRUISE SHIPS AND PASSENGERS WHICH CALLED IN 2002 COMPARED WITH 2003

2002 CRUISE SHIPS — PASSENGERS

RMS *St Helena*	22 January	90 passengers landed
MV *Bremen*	4 March	65 passengers landed
MV *Europa*	14 January	205 passengers; did not land
MV *Bremen*	4 March	65 passengers landed
MV *Endeavour*	17 March	64 passengers landed
MV *Molchanov*	2 April	54 passengers landed
MV *Explorer*	25 October	70 passengers landed
MV *Endeavour*	2 November	68 passengers landed

2003 CRUISE SHIPS — PASSENGERS

MV *Astoria*	16 February	300 passengers; did not land
RMS *St Helena*	21 January	85 passengers landed
MV *Astoria*	6 February	300 passengers; did not land
MS *Hanseatic*	4 February	70 passengers landed
MV *Endeavour*	15 March	56 passengers; only 36 landed
MV *Molchanov*	1 April	48 passengers landed
MV *Orion*	7 December	65 passengers; only 30 landed
MV *Royal Princess*	24 December	1,200 Passengers; did not land

CREWING A LONGBOAT TO NIGHTINGALE

[This chapter is dedicated to my late father-in-law Stephen Glass]

The sound of the gong being rung at 06.00 announces the start of a fishing day. The sky is clear with several puffy white clouds about, looking like balls of cotton wool. A few of the fishermen are already on their way down to the harbour, eager to get away fishing as soon as possible. A dozen men or more are standing in front of Allan Green's house. My father and I join them. We are going to decide if today would be a good day to sail across to Nightingale.

Allan's house is situated in the middle of the village, and is the usual place for the men to meet to plan a trip to Nightingale. He turns to my father and asks: "What do you make of the wind, Spike?" My father answers, "This wind is north west. Look, the bottom cloud is passing Big Point." Big Point is a large ridge that rises from sea level 2,000 feet to the first base. It's the furthest point one can see looking east from the village.

Everyone looks east towards Big Point. A cloud drifts past it, out of sight. Harold Green says, "The sea breeze is setting in on Hottentot Point. It's going to be a bully day for Nightingale." Stanley Swain (our coxswain) says, "Well, what are we waiting for? There are enough men here to crew four boats." Allan concludes, "Yes! Let's be off, there's not going to be much wind, the glass is hanging steady."

The coxswains of the longboats have already made arrangements a week earlier with their crews to see which people will be going. As usual, some of the original crew will not be going, but some men from the other boats go instead to make up the numbers. We leave en masse to pack up our gear; my wife Sharon's father, Stephen Glass, calls to Allan, "Don't forget the keys to the shack!" Allan nods as he hurries away. At home we pack up our gear and carry it down to the edge of the road for the tractor to pick up. A few tractors will be driven throughout the village, the drivers stopping outside the houses, which have bags of potatoes, cans of water, boxes of groceries, kit bags, wood, sails, and ropes. This is all piled on to the trailers. When they are fully laden, the drivers head for the field next to the school to take one of the longboats in tow. The crew will walk either side of the boat, holding to the gunwales keeping it on an even keel.

All the men who are going to Nightingale will have had their gear packed and ready several days before the actual trip occurs. At home my father and I carry our gear down to the road. I fill the 20 litre cans with drinking water, while he gets the boat's equipment. We will be sailing across to Nightingale in our longboat *Raffee* which we share with six other men. My father is one of the coxswains of the boat, but since reaching the age of 65, he has now left the responsibility of boat repairs and maintenance of the sails to Stanley Swain, who is now the senior coxswain for *Raffee*.

As soon as we have finished at home, we head down to get the boats ready to take down to the harbour, leaving the women packing a rucksack with our lunch for the trip. The women will bring this to the harbour and wait until the boats have been loaded, before passing the bags on to their husbands. It's the last cargo to be placed into the boat.

When we get to where the boats are kept, all the men work together as a team of 12 to 20 persons turning the boat upright, then lifting the stern, then the bow, amid shouts of "Now, up with her." Stephen (known as Smiley because of his infectious grin), the hat on his head at a jaunty angle, shouts as he pulls on *Britannia*'s bow rope. "Come on, Anderson," he says, "show your strength. Keep going, it's only a bit further." Grinning, he gives Anderson Green (who is one of *Britannia*'s crew) a wink. We keep pulling until the boat is finally ready to be towed by the tractor. At the harbour, the boat is lifted into the water by crane. These boats are made of glass fibre and weigh about 1,100 kilos; it is about ten metres in length, with a beam of 2.5 metres.

When the boat is in the water, each crew member will collect his gear from the trailer and pile it on the quay, next to where his boat is moored. While four of the crew load the boat, the other two will collect the oars, boom, and mast and tie the sail onto the gaff boom.

Loading the boat is a precarious task. The coxswain and one crew member will carefully place the cargo in it, so with all the cargo loaded, the boat will be at a level trim, to obtain maximum speed when sailing. The heaviest items are loaded first, usually the 25 litre cans of water, sacks of potatoes and wood. This is placed each side of the keel from the mast step back to the third thwart from the stern. Other lighter items of cargo are evenly placed between the cans and sacks throughout the boat. Once this has been completed, in comes the oars, mast, boom and sail.

With the loading finished, the crew scramble into the boat, ship the rudder and oars, and row out of the harbour, and moor to the kelp about one hundred metres from the point of the west break water. They will proceed to put up the mast, tighten the backstays, and prepare the jib and sail for hoisting. From then on it is just a matter of waiting for all the boats to row out of the harbour and ready their sails for hoisting. As soon as the last boat comes out of the harbour and is ready for hoisting its sail, the senior coxswain gives a signal to the other crews and the men stand as one and give a mighty shout of "Hip, Hip, HOOOORAAAY!" Each waving their hats to accompany the three cheers, given as a way of saying goodbye to the people onshore.

The women wave back, some of them waving white hankies, as they stand lining the harbour road along the edge of the cliff east of the fishing factory. The women will wait patiently for a few more minutes to wave goodbye to their loved ones; they will not leave the harbour area until the traditional farewell has been given. It's our way of saying Bon Voyage (until we meet again).

As the boats hoist sail, the women turn without a backward glance and hurry back to their jobs. Before the boats leave the harbour, the Harbour Master will pick one of the coxswains to act as senior coxswain for the entire trip. His job is to make sure the fleet sails together for safety and will have the last words in debates if the weather conditions are right for any boat to sail from Nightingale back to Tristan. A head count will be taken of all people going to Nightingale and given to the Administrator who will put up a notice announcing which boats have gone to Nightingale, who is coxswain, crew and passengers on the boats. Each boat carries flare, torches, fishing lines, matches, and VHF radios. One of the coxswain or crew will take the main radio set along with two first aid boxes supplied by the doctor. Hourly radio contact will be kept between the longboats and Tristan Radio until they reach Nightingale.

The rest of the men back on Tristan eagerly monitor the news of the boats' progress. There will be much speculation on which will be the first to win the race to Nightingale. Each has their own tenacious beliefs that their boat is the fastest on the fleet, many a heated debate having taken place among the island men on this subject. When the longboats get to Nightingale, radio contact will be made with Tristan radio twice a day, at 08.00 and at 16.00.

With sails hoisted they head towards Nightingale, passing the familiar landmarks of Herald Point, Hill Piece and The Patches. The boats began gathering speed as they sail pass Anchorstock Point as the wind becomes stronger.

As soon as we have finished hoisting the sails, the coxswain will tell the crew where to sit in the boat, either before or after the mast, usually sitting one person on each thwart from mast to the stern off the boat. On the stern sheets he will have the passengers sitting. It will take anything from three to five hours to reach Nightingale, depending on the strength of the wind. If there is a moderate breeze about 15 knots, the boats move over the sea at a leisurely rate. The halyards are secured to the thwart and everyone enjoys the ride, and takes it in turns steering the boat under the eagle eye of the coxswain, who is forever watching the boat's trim.

If the wind is blowing at 25 knots, the coxswain will steer the boat himself, and the most experienced crew member tends the halyards, holding on to them after taking a rolling turn around the thwart in case of a sudden gust of wind that could cause the boat to broach, he would be able to lower the sail in a matter of seconds. It's very exhilarating to sail a longboat in this amount of breeze with a following sea. First the bow dips into the sea, the water running level with the gunnels, so only the stem of the boat is sticking out of the water. As the boat gathers momentum, being pushed by the wind and waves, the bow then picks up as the boat surfs down the waves, bringing the spray right back to the mast, causing a small rainbow over the bow. The boat will surf down three to five waves in succession as the coxswain steers her from one wave to the next. By now the boat will be surfing at such a speed, the jib and sail will have fallen slack having the wind taken out of them by the speed of the surfing boat. As the boat surfs off the last wave, the coxswain lets (tip) or luff slightly into the wind to fill the sails again and catch the next set of waves. Sometimes the lee gunwale (the side of the boat on which the sail is carried) runs level with the water; it almost seems that the boat will overturn, but in the blink of an eye the coxswain rights the boat and is off surfing down the waves.

Passing Anchorstock we encounter the fishing boats whose crews shout encouragement to us or, maybe, they'll be pulling the leg of a friend in the boat. Leaving the fishing boats behind, we sail on at a steady rate, *Raffee* overtaking the other boats. As we pass the *Canton*, I shout across to Harold to ask if he needs a tow (Harold and I are always betting on whose longboat can sail the fastest). Harold's response is to sail *Canton* close to *Raffee,* taking the wind out of our sail. "Cheat," I shout across to him, but Harold only laughs and winks at me knowing that he has the upper hand for the moment: 20 minutes later we are still under *Canton*'s lee, although sailing at times slightly ahead of her.

Harold, who is a very experienced coxswain shouts across to Stan, "We should wait for the other boats." We lower sail to wait as the other boats close in on us. *Raffee* draws slightly ahead of *Canton*, as we have the advantage of a bigger jib. As the other boats drew abreast of us, Stan gives the order to hoist the sail. As soon as the sail is up, Stan lets *Raffee* luff to get windward of *Canton*. The wind is gusting more and *Raffee* canters along. There will be no catching her now: she has the bit in her teeth, rushing over the blue sea and sun dazzled waves like a sprinted filly reacting lively to the movement of the waves.

I remember my first trip to Nightingale in a longboat as crew. I had left school at the age of 15 and started work at the fishing factory. Two weeks later I was on my way to Nightingale. It was a lovely day with hardly any wind. The sun shining down on the sea out of a cloudless blue sky; the boats rolling lazily on the swell, moving forward ever so slowly. The creaking of the backstays, the slap of the sails, the smell of canvas and salt making me feel rather sick, as a few of us lounged on the thwarts at times dozing off, only to be brought back to reality by someone starting a feeble conversation.

"It's a lovely day on the water. Just the sort of day to bring women and children across." Then silence, followed by "Margaret Rose is coming along much better now." Silence. "The boats are sailing close together. Like this, you won't have to wait." Silence again. "I don't say the boats up the windward ain't got more wind." Dougie, stood up by the mast, looks out and says, "There's a bit more darker water up ahead." Silence again, followed by Dougie whistling a catchy tune. Sogneas looks at me questioningly and says "Hey Sonny, I don't say you're feeling half sick!" "No, I'm fine," I protest vehemently, sitting up much straighter. Soggy, as he was called by the islanders, looks at me and grins knowingly.

Soggy sadly passed away in Cape Town where he was undergoing an operation, while travelling to his son's wedding in England. He will always be remembered by *Raffee*'s crew as the best jib man they had. He always had an amicable grin on his face, and was a strong supporter of *Raffee*, even going as far as to bet his friends a sheep that *Raffee* would be the first boat to reach Nightingale. One can hear him now rapping loudly on a tin plate in front of his cooking hut on Nightingale shouting to his shack mates Herbert and Lewis, "Munchy, Munchy, grub up, come and get it." He was one of those rare people who never complained or had a bad word to say about fellow islanders.

We reached Nightingale at midday. *Raffee* was the first boat there, it was quite nice at the landing. We had just started to unload *Raffee* when the other boats arrived. *Britannia*, *British Flag* and *Canton* all drop sail within a boat length of each other although it looked like *Britannia* had the edge over the other two. "What kept you?" I call out to Harold, who retorts, "It would have been a different story if you did not have the big jib. Why, it's half the size of our main sail." "That's no excuse," I answer. "Well, give it to me on our way back. Then we'll see the difference," replies Harold, knowing full well that I would never agree to give *Canton* the advantage.

The debate stops short as we are both busy with the unloading. The coxswain of each boat will guide it with a steering oar, during unloading, while one of the crew puts another oar in to back the boat out if needed. When the cargo has been unloaded and the boats are pulled up on to the rock and secured, each person carries their luggage up to their shacks. It will take several journeys back and forth to bring all the gear up.

These shacks are built from local stone, roughly about 3.5 metres square with an asbestos roof and the insides lined with hardboard. Two or three men will share two shacks, one for sleeping, and the other for cooking. They are quite crudely built, but dry and comfortable inside. The sleeping shack will have a couple of single beds, a cupboard for stores and maybe a small table. All bed linen is taken over each trip; almost everyone uses a sheet and a sleeping bag. The cooking shack has a built in chimney with a fireplace for cooking, a small sink, cupboard and table. Two long benches are used as seats, most have an earth floor. A few have a two-burner gas stove. All the cooking is done over an open fire using chopped down *Phylica arborea* – better known as 'island wood trees' which grow there. To get this wood, we have to walk up a fairly steep slope, about two miles through a path in the tussock, to the hill on which the wood grows. We cut down eight or ten lengths of tree limbs, as thick as a man's upper arm and two metres long, tie these into a bundle, stuff one side with ferns, to make it soft against our backs, then put it on to our backs and trek back down to the shacks.

As soon as we are finished with our luggage, there's just enough time to grab a cup of tea and a sandwich, then it is off into the penguin rookeries which are located among the two metre tussock grass to fill up guano, which is used as a fertilizer when planting our potatoes. Each man will fill four to five sacks to take back to Tristan in the boat, each vessel will carry 30 sacks. A garden rake or fork is used to gather the guano into mounds, about a metre wide and half a metre high. This will usually fill one sack. While my father and Ernest Repetto (Ernie as he is called) scoop up the guano, I fill the sacks, tie up the tops and carry them out of the tussock onto the path. This is back breaking work, which takes us until 17.00. With just the last sacks to fill, I start carrying them to the rock where the boats are. They will be left there until we return to Tristan and it is close by for loading when needed.

Once clear of the tussock, a man can usually carry two sacks tied together. By the time I finished carrying the two sacks of guano, Ernie has hunted half a dozen young shearwaters, taking them from their burrows under the tussock. He skins and dresses them.

My father has a good fire going, the new potatoes are already on the boil. Soon the smell of fried petrels and onions wafts through on the evening air. The other people will have a similar meal tonight. I join Ernie and my father in the cooking shack; a single candle and the glow from the fire cast dim soft shadows about the place reflecting on each of their faces as it light the interior. Ernie looks up as I enter the shack and asks, "Do you want some tea?" "Yes," I reply, and he hands me a freshly brewed mug, then disappears, only to return a few moments later with some beers which he passed to us saying with a grin, "Must have the night cap!"

Sipping the beer, my thoughts drift back to the first time I came as crew to Nightingale and Ernie taught me to hunt petrels. After several attempts, I did not have any petrels. "Connie, you must put all your arm into the hole, right up to the shoulder and keep your leg in the air." Yeah, right, I thought, not believing a word. But after trying this out - at least, excluding the bit about the leg - in no time I had caught a dozen birds. "Didn't I told you so," Ernie remarked. I did not answer but just grinned sheepishly.

My father and Ernie were swapping yarns of trips to Nightingale when they were young men. It was very interesting to listen to them relate encounters from the past in sombre tones, the sincerity of memories reflecting on their faces. When supper was finished we went to bed tired out by the day's events. The next morning I awoke to the sound of the sea washing onto the rocks below. The penguins were calling in their quaint tones. In the background was the thud, thud of someone chopping wood for the fire.

After a late breakfast, I walked up onto the hill for a bundle of wood, while Ernie and my father carried out some maintenance to the shack; 45 minutes later and rather out of breath, I reached the top of the hill where the wood grew. (This was before it was destroyed by the hurricane in 2001). I told passengers from the cruise ships that this was called the 'Enchanted Wood'. Once you entered under the trees, the place had a magic tranquil aura about it. It was one of the beauties of God's creation. The trees grow to about five to six metres high, which is unusual for *Phylica arborea*. Tussock grass and a natural rockery stand among the lush green ferns and bog grass encloses it. The yellow nosed albatross, shearwaters, thrush and bunting all have their nests built there. In the space of a few minutes you can see all four species of birds, flying and walking about, oblivious to human presence. Shafts of sunlight shine through the trees, creating sunbeams. Such is the feel of the place, it seems all that were missing were the fairies and elves dancing in between the glades. To add to this enchantment, is a spectacular view looking out over the middle islands of Alex Island and Stoltenhoff Island; Tristan and Inaccessible were standing a deep blue on the horizon.

I stayed there for a while enjoying the views. Then, I lifted the bundle of wood on my back and set off down to the shacks. I got back to find my father breaking up wood for the fire, and Ernie was fishing off the rocks. He had already caught several large five fingers. This evening it will be fish and chips for supper. On Nightingale we tend to cook two meals a day.

While waiting for lunch, I visit Stephen (my father-in-law) to see if there are any chores I can help him with. I find him and Allan sitting in their sleeping shack drinking a beer, having just finished re-nailing its front. "Come in, Johnny, take a seat," he says, grinning (he usually calls most younger men 'Johnny' as a way of greeting them). "Would you like tot?"

"I will have a beer please if you got it," I replied. He opens a cupboard by his bed, rummages inside and passes me a beer. "Do you have anything to carry down on the rock or bring up?" I ask, opening the beer.

"Only a bag of guano and a can of water," he says.

"Leave them. I will sort it out later," I reply.

Stephen is five feet five inches in height, but is very energetic; an excellent carpenter and a coxswain. He was passed as a longboat coxswain at the age of 23, such was his skill as a seamen. Now he has passed the responsibility on to Allan Swain who is *Britannia*'s senior coxswain. Stephen passed away in 2000 while in Cape Town for medical treatment. He practically helped every family on the island at some time with maintenance of their houses. He was never known to say 'no' to anyone who asked for his help. I was very fond of him: his grandson Leon was the apple of his eye. We still miss him very much, especially on a Sunday, when he would visit us, regular as clockwork. He was a strong, forthright character, who served several terms as a councillor on the island.

I finish drinking the beer and leave Stephen and Allan preparing their lunch. I pick up the sack of guano to take down on the rock and bring back the can of water. On the way back with the water, my father calls that lunch was ready. I return to find Ernie and my father already tucking into theirs with gusto.

Lunch is about 11.30 and supper around 17.00; breakfast is usually a sandwich and a cup of tea. If one needs a bath there are several pools of salt or 'alum' water, this is fresh water that soaks through the ground on Nightingale and runs out onto the rocks. It's not good for drinking but is known to heal any cuts or rashes very quickly.

People on Nightingale will catch crayfish off the rocks, using a hoop net. I set off after lunch to try my luck, within an hour or so I have caught several for supper. It's my turn to cook. I will make some crayfish hash. When I get back I find Ernie and Stephen playing a game of cards while my father looks on. Stephen reckons it's going to rain. He is right: after supper it starts. There is a chill in the air; it looks like the wind will change to the south.

Next morning, everyone is up early. The wind has backed to the south, and is very light. The sky and sea reflecting a pale washed grey. 08.00: radio contact is made with Tristan. They also have the wind light from the south. The coxswains decided to return home and have asked for the launch to be on stand by, in case we need a tow. Soon everyone is busy working as a team carrying the cargo down and pushing the boats into the water and loading them. 10.00: we hoist sail and head back to Tristan, the boats sailing close together, first one taking the lead, as she gets a bit more wind, but it's still light. As the head boat loses the wind, another boat passes her until her sail is hanging slack. This process goes on for a couple of hours, then the wind dies off altogether. The sea looks like glass, without a ripple, the odd ground swell was now drifting with the current.

Each boat puts a couple of oars out and we start to row slowly, taking breaks of ten minutes. We carry on until the launch, which has to be called by the senior coxswain, takes us in tow. We are about halfway between Tristan and Nightingale. There will be no race back today.

As the launch sets off with the boats behind, we settle down with some Coke and orangeade sent by our families on the launch. One of the crew passes around pieces of fruit cake. I looked back at Nightingale growing smaller in the distance, wondering if the penguins are glad that the brief human intrusion is over, or whether we were just another mammal in their small world.

THE *CANTON'S* LAST VOYAGE TO NIGHTINGALE

Thursday, 4th April 2002 dawned with a clear sky; a light wind was blowing from the north. After several weeks of waiting, the islanders decided today would be a good day to sail across to Nightingale on the fatting trip. It would be the first time many of the men had been to Nightingale since the storm on 21st May 2001. They were taking extra building materials to mend their huts.

The six longboats going across to Nightingale were *Raffee, Margaret Rose, Stirling Castle, British Flag, Britannia,* and *Canton*. From 08.00 onwards, the village was abuzz with people rushing to and fro, with a constant stream of vehicles taking stores to the harbour. By 09.00 the longboats had been pulled down to the harbour and hoisted into the water, where their crews were busy loading the cargo.

Duncan Lavarello and I were taking the Police RIB out, with the Administrator (Bill Dickson) and Norman Glass to take some photos. At 10.40 all the boats had left the harbour and were hoisting their sails off Herald Point. We set off towards Anchorstock, keeping just ahead of the boats, taking photos as they sailed passed the RIB. By 11.00, the boats had sailed pass Anchorstock Point. The wind was starting to increase as the sea breeze set in; the sky had become more overcast with the wind shifting to the north east, bringing a scattering of rain. Duncan remarked if it kept on raining, the wind would increase and the boats were in for a rough trip. At 11.30 there was a light drizzle of rain. The boats were about six miles off Anchorstock, encountering very confused seas, 1½ to 2 metres high. It was about a force 3-4 sea state; the wind was increasing quite quickly, gusting 30 to 35 knots.

The fleet sailed by surfing down the waves, with *Stirling Castle* and *Raffee* leading the race; the others following close behind. We kept along with them for about another mile, the leading boats were lowering their sails. At first it seemed they were waiting for the others, but we saw that all of the boats were taking in the big jibs to replace them with a smaller storm jib. On closer inspection, we saw that some of the boats were reefing the main sails into the second reef. During this time, the fleet had become more separated over an area of about half a square mile. I had just turned to Duncan, who was standing up behind the steering consul of the RIB to say we should be heading home, when Duncan suddenly pointed and said, "Look, there is a couple of men waving life jackets on one of the boats." At first I could not see them because they were quite a way off. However, the boat was soon identified to be *Canton*, which was at the back of the fleet. We quickly shot off to see what was the matter.

Moments later, we drew alongside *Canton*, where we found the crew frantically bailing and pumping water from the boat. They said they were caught unawares by the combination of a sudden gust of wind and a freak wave, which threw the boat over onto its side, so the lee gunwale was under the water. One must bear in mind these are open hulled boats. Caught momentarily by surprise, the crew reacted quickly by lowering the main sail, righting the boat up again. This happened when they were in the process of changing their big jib for a smaller one.

Harold Green, one of the coxswains, asked if we would keep the RIB alongside until they had the boat bailed out, as there might be a chance of another wave breaking into *Canton*, as she was lying at an angle to the oncoming waves. *Canton*, at this time, had less freeboard from the top of the gunwale to the water line than the RIB. I asked them if they would like us to help them bail, to which they said "Yes". After conferring with the others, Duncan and Norman jumped into *Canton* and helped with the bailing. Bill offered to help, but I needed him to be in the RIB just in case anything happened. Norman and Duncan were in the boat standing up to their knees in water as they bailed, with loose cargo floating between the thwarts. Meanwhile John Lavarello and Kevin Glass set about hoisting a storm jib, so they could get some steerage way on the boat and would not be wallowing at the mercy of the seas. Soon John and Kevin had the jib hoisted and I could see that *Canton* was riding much higher in the water, in fact now there was no fear of her being swamped by the waves.

Bill and I set off with the RIB to let the other crews know what had happened. I asked the coxswain of each boat to keep a listening watch on their VHF hand held radios. The fact that *Canton*'s crew had to shift some cargo to get the boat bailed out would not help matters, as the boat would be out of trim for sailing. On arrival back at *Canton*, we saw that the bailing had been completed, although the cargo was wet, especially the crews' clothes. Duncan and Norman got back into the RIB and the boats hoisted sail again. We followed them for about ten minutes by which time the waves had increased to about four metres in height.

12.30: with our fuel running low, we turned back towards Tristan, making a run for The Caves. We arrived off The Caves at 13.10 and continued on to Stony Beach, where after a brief stop, we returned to the harbour by way of Sandy Point. We ran into a strong head wind gusting at such strength it caused what we call willies: whirling downdrafts of wind which are capable of overturning a boat. The only way to cope with these down-drafts is to point the bow of the RIB into them, with extra weight forward and have just enough power for steerage, thus keeping the boat as low in the water as possible. We arrived at the harbour at 14.00 to learn that the longboats reached Nightingale safely.

The following morning at 08.30, when the daily contact was made with Nightingale by radio, a most traumatic story was heard. This account of what happened is from the people who were there.

The longboats reached Nightingale around 14.00; *Raffee* was the first boat to arrive. By then the wind had increased more. At the landing rock, there was quite a swell running from the east, fuelled by a short choppy sea. From the moment the boats arrived, it was difficult to keep them moored. The thing to do is to tie a couple of ropes to the kelp, which acts as a mooring. There is usually a large bed of kelp growing around Nightingale, but as fate would have it, the kelp was rotten and the boats kept breaking their mooring and started to drift away. A couple of men who were put ashore had tied a rope from the shore to one of the boats, then the others tied up behind, except *British Flag*, whose crew had 'a night to remember'.

British Flag was the third boat to arrive at Nightingale. She had quite a young crew, a couple of whom were a bit inexperienced. Barney Swain was the coxswain of *British Flag* for the trip; this information is drawn from his account. They had dropped sail about 14.15. By then, it was raining steadily. After several unsuccessful attempts to moor the boat to kelp, they found the strong wind was blowing the boat away from the rock. They tried to row back, breaking an oar in the process. Alas, the wind was too strong for them to row against and getting the oars caught in the kelp made the task difficult.

Having only four oars, but now left with just three, Barney took the safe option and instructed his crew to hoist the jib, saying they were going to sail to the lee at The Old Landing Place, which is about one and a half miles east of the main landing rock. This was to avoid being blown away from Nightingale. They got to the lee at 15.00 and moored the boat to some kelp a safe distance from shore. The crew were wet and it was still raining in the lee, but they changed into dry clothes, put on oilskin suits and had some hot tea.

When it got dark, they took turns to keep an anchor watch. The crew consisted of Adrian and Nicky Swain and Grant and Desmond Green. At 22.00, the boat broke from its mooring to the kelp. With the wind coming up from the east, Barney told the crew to hoist the gaff boom with a small section of the main sail and they sailed back towards the main landing rock, getting as far as Cook's Beach. Because the night was very dark, they had to keep a safe distance from shore. From Cook's Beach, they rowed to the shelter of Alex Island about a mile away, and a quarter of a mile west of the main landing rock. At midnight they arrived in the shelter of Alex Island. It was calmer now and the sea was much smoother. They secured the boat and settled down for the rest of the night. More than a few prayers were offered up for their safekeeping.

07.00 on Friday 5th April, the *British Flag* was at the landing rock and with the help of the other men on Nightingale, they soon had the boat pulled on to the rock. That night at the main landing there was another drama unfolding, as the *British Flag* sailed for the lee at The Old Landing Place. The other crews saw the plight of the *British Flag* and put a double crew of 12 men into *Britannia* and set off to help.

They only got about 40 metres from the mooring, when they had to turn back, because the wind was too strong for them. On turning back, they had to row double, two men to each oar, to achieve maximum power. They got to the mooring, rowing five oars, breaking another one getting there.

The unloading of the boat cargo was soon under way. Three men were left in each boat, which would take it in turn to come to the landing to be unloaded. Once unloaded, they would move back to the mooring, until the last boat had been unloaded. This was a slow process, as a couple of men had to have a rope tied around their waist to be kept from being washed off the rock, as they caught the cargo from the boats and passed it onto the rock. Several times they were awash with water up to their waist, as the boats could only be unloaded between sets of waves. The boat that was being unloaded would have to be backed away from the rock when a nasty set of waves approached.

19.30: as it was getting dark, the unloading was completed. Darkness was approaching fast and everyone was wet and weary. The men had to face the daunting task of pulling the boats onto the rock. *Stirling Castle* was the first boat to be pulled on to the rock. Next it was *Canton*'s turn, but the men could not get her pulled onto the rock. She started to take water over her stern and had to be pushed back to the mooring to be pumped out again. *Raffee* was pulled up next but only after a couple of attempts were made.

Then it was *Canton*'s turn again, with three extra men on the rock, the job should be more easier. But it was not to be. Again, fate dealt a final blow. As *Canton* was being pulled onto the rock a large freak wave appeared out of the gathering darkness and broke over the stern, filling the boat with water

Now it was impossible to pull the boat on to the rock with all that water on board. Once more, *Canton* was let into the sea, but unfortunately with the weight of the water and no buoyancy to compensate for it, *Canton* began to sink stern first. With another huge wave looming, the men shouted to Roger Glass, who was manning the steering oar, to jump for his life, to avoid being washed overboard. Roger made it on to the rock just in the nick of time. Five minutes later, *Canton* had sunk. The painter (bow rope) was the only thing that was still attached to the boat. This was fastened to the rock, in the hope that

Canton could be pulled up again. The men were stunned to silence, but there was nothing they could do. They could not believe that a glass fibre boat could sink so quickly.

Because of the darkness, the men worked by torchlight. The men on the rock shouted to the crews left in *Margaret Rose* and *Britannia* to all get into one boat. The *Britannia*'s crew got into *Margaret Rose* and left *Britannia* at the mooring. *Margaret Rose* was pulled on to the rock with less effort than the other boats. Suddenly, someone shouted *Britannia* had broken from the mooring and was drifting back on to a reef. By now, the men were at the end of their tether, but Herbert Glass ran across the rock, got hold of the only mooring rope and started to pull *Britannia* away from the reef. Allan Swain, the coxswain of *Britannia*, shouted to the others that they would bring the boat to the rock and try to get her pulled up onto the rock, maybe preventing another accident. Quickly, *Britannia* was pulled to the rock, coming in at a straight line, despite the strong wind. It was as if some unseen helmsmen was steering her. After a final effort, *Britannia* was hauled to safety with only the bottom of the hull scarred to show for it.

22.00: cold, wet and tired, the men made their way to their huts, having made the boats secure. No one could really sleep that night, thinking about the crew of the *British Flag*.

Around 01.30, 74-year-old Allan Green, the oldest crew member on Nightingale, spotted the light of the *British Flag* going towards Alex Island. He informed Neil Swain, who tried to call Barney on VHF but got no answer. Neil then tried flashing his torch so that Barney knew that the people on Nightingale had seen them. Barney flashed the torch back in acknowledgement to Neil's signal.

Later, I heard of another incident that could have ended in disaster. It was soon after we had left the boats. *Britannia*'s rudder broke while she was still under sail, surfing down a wave. During this time, Neil Swain was steering the boat. He said they were riding on top of a huge wave with the boat surfing along at about 12 knots. Suddenly, he felt the pressure come off the tiller and it went slack. Knowing something was wrong, he shouted to Allan Swain to lower the sail at once. Luckily *Britannia* kept on a straight course. She could have easily turned into the oncoming seas and broached. On checking, Neil found the rudder had broken off above the top spindle. All boats carry a spare rudder in case of such an event, but to get one changed and fitted again, in a confused sea, is no mean task.

The rudders are two metres long 25 mm thick and 50 cm wide, weighing about 25 kilos. They have two steel pins about 8 mm in diameter and 15 cm long. These are attached to the rudder about 60 cm apart. In the stern of the boat there are two steel rings into which the spindles fit. To fit the spare rudder on, Neil said they tied a rope on top to steady it, while he sat astride the stern sheets to guide the rudder in place. Despite the rolling of the boat, Neil got the rudder into the rings on the first try. Soon they had hoisted sail and were racing along after the other boats to Nightingale.

On Tristan the next day, the Fisheries Patrol boat *Wave Dancer*, was made ready to take supplies and oars to Nightingale and maybe get *Canton* off the sea bed, but this was not to be. The *Wave Dancer* sailed for Nightingale amid an increasing north-west storm. In hindsight, the only thing that would have prevented *Canton* sinking was if the winch which we are getting on Tristan had been installed. Manpower had not been sufficient to get the boat on to the rock when the extra weight of the water had to be contended with.

On Tuesday 10th April, the *Wave Dancer* and the Police RIB left for Nightingale again with more supplies for the people there, and to try to have another go at rescuing *Canton*. The *Wave Dancer* crew took a winch to help with the task. Duncan and I loaded up the RIB and put the spare outboard on for extra power. We left the harbour at 07.30. The wind was light, from the west. About one mile off Anchorstock Point, Duncan pointed to a blue bucket that was floating about 10 metres off our starboard side. Later, we heard this bucket belonging to Kevin, had drifted all the way from Nightingale, having been washed out of *Canton* when she sank. I did not stop to pick it up, for fear of getting some of our cargo wet by the spray.

After arriving at Nightingale, we found that we could not land our cargo at the rock because there was too much swell running. The cargo had to be unloaded at the West Side landing rocks. This spot is the best place to land passengers from cruise ships. Soon the *Wave Dancer* arrived and was at anchor. It took a couple of trips in the RIB to ferry her cargo to the west landing. While Duncan helped with the cargo onshore, James Glass and I went with the RIB back to the main landing. We looked at the prospect of getting *Canton* up using the winch. But it was to no avail, there was too much swell running to achieve this task.

Jack Green, the senior coxswain for the trip, said that they had seen a couple of her thwarts with the mast-board attached floating off the rock the day before we arrived. It appeared that the inside of Canton was being broken up by the strong surge of the current. Looking down into the water, which is about seven metres deep, it had a bluish tinge to it. I could just see the white shimmering outline of *Canton* laying on the sea bed, like some ghostly apparition that one sees in the illustrations of the *Flying Dutchma*n. It was then I realised with a feeling of nostalgia that the fabled *Canton*, a name that had been given to generations of longboats, had made her last voyage to Nightingale, never to return to her home port on Tristan.

I wondered if her crew would build another longboat, and would they name it *Canton*? After we left Nightingale at 13.00 I had mixed feelings. Given the present way of life on Tristan, *Canton*'s crew may decide it's not financially worth building another longboat.

Following the safe return of the longboats on 18th April, a meeting was held with all the longboat coxswains, the Administrator and myself (as Head of Search and Rescue). This led to the safety regulations being updated. The outcome was new life jackets for all people going to Nightingale by boat must be worn, new VHF waterproof marine multi-channel radios, new flares, the possibility of more buoyancy to be put in the boats, a new Rescue RIB to accompany the boats to Nightingale, or to be on standby if needed. All this was instigated with the help of Bill Dickson, who was then the Administrator. He's no stranger to the sea, having served time in the Royal Marines and he holds a Yacht Master's Certificate. At this point I would like to thank him on behalf of all the longboat crews for all his help and support in getting the items needed for their safety.

A few weeks after the boats got back from Nightingale, a plastic bag containing waterproof coats with John Lavarello's name on, was picked up at The Caves. It had been cast up on the beach by the pond. This bag was washed out of *Canton* at one stage during the voyage. Looking at the overall view of this incident, things could have been worse if it was not for the skill and seamanship of the Tristanian men, who are second to none in their boat handling.

I believe it's to this and the will of God that a worse scenario did not occur.

LEGENDS OF TRISTAN

This is a collection of short stories told to me by my grandparents, uncles and parents. As with most stories, they are based on fact, but they have been passed down from one generation to the next, so over the years some of the facts may have been distorted or a little fiction added. This is how I think the events took place. In some stories it is up to the reader to make up their own mind. This chapter, I would like to dedicate to the memory of my late Uncle Nelson Green, who kept me enthralled with his tales of the past, told with such clarity of detail.

THOMAS CURRIE'S KETTLE

27th December 1810 was a sunny day. The small sailing lugger *Baltic* on passage from Rio de Janeiro, put ashore on Tristan da Cunha three men, Jonathan Lambert, Tomasso Corri (anglicised as Thomas Currie and by which name we will refer to him in this story) and Andrew Millet, with an assortment of livestock, vegetable seeds, and fruit trees. This unlikely trio of rogues had with them a huge iron chest. The crew of the *Baltic* was convinced that the chest contained treasure: loot gained from the three men's' wild affrays upon the Spanish Main as part of a group of buccaneers, although Lambert (as captain of the group) claimed they were once privateers preying on British, Spanish and French merchant shipping. Whatever they might have been, they appear to have been in league with pirates and wanted to make a fresh break from their colourful past. Their plan was to farm the land on Tristan, growing enough fresh fruit, vegetables and meat to supply passing ships in exchange for money or other items that they did not have.

However this project was doomed from the start, no matter how industrious they seemed. They did not take into account the harsh weather conditions. They did manage to grow a substantial amount of produce, but not on the scale they had hoped for. Crews of American privateers took most of their livestock during the war with Britain in 1812. The men tried for two years on Tristan to make a go of things, and were joined by another American by the name of Williams, no doubt a fellow from their privateering days.

When HMS *Semiramis* called at Tristan on the 5th March 1813, they found Currie to be the only inhabitant. He told Captain Richardson that Lambert, Williams and Millet had taken their boat out fishing and had not returned. He assumed the boat must have capsized and they all drowned.

Some time later, Currie was joined by two more Americans - John Tankard and John Telson, most likely more of his privateer shipmates. In 1814, a Spanish youth, one Bistino Poncho Camilla, from an English ship, agreed to throw in his lot with Currie and to work with him for two years. The four carried on the work started by Lambert, but Telson and Tankard also mysteriously disappeared between 1815 and 1816.

When the British sent a garrison to annex Tristan against the possibility of the French using it as a base from which to free Napoleon from St Helena, only Currie and Bastino greeted them at the beach on 14th August 1816. One of the soldiers from the garrison, a Corporal William Glass, was to have a profound effect in the history of Tristan when the garrison returned to Cape Town almost two years later. With the arrival of the garrison, Currie had access to their canteen, where he bought grog paid for with gold coins. In his bouts of drunkenness, he hinted that he had buried treasure and that he had sorted out Lambert, Williams and Millet, because they wanted to take it. When asked about Tankard and Telson, he grinned, saying they were still in search of the Lambert treasure chest. No one knew of the whereabouts of the treasure he kept hidden in a huge copper kettle, which he would only tell his best friend where it was kept.

From then on, the soldiers tried to get Currie to reveal his secret. He told them it was somewhere between the two waterfalls. Whether this was true or not, no one ever knew even though many soldiers tried to follow Currie when he went to get more coins to pay for his grog. On 27th September 1817, he had a stroke just as he was about to reveal his secret to William Glass and another soldier.

After his death the gunners spent a lot of time searching and digging for Currie's chest or copper kettle, but to this day, nothing has ever been found. Maybe the 1961 volcanic eruption has covered this spot; then in that case, the treasure is lost forever. To this day Tristanians still tell their children how they would love to find Currie's copper kettle, filled with gold coins from the Spanish Main.

A PIECE OF BREAD AND WATER PLEASE

Since Tristan was discovered in 1506, there have been many ships wrecked on her cliff bound shores. Many sailors whose ships were wrecked on the south coast of the island, not only had to survive the shipwreck, but had to reach the settlement on the north shore, either by climbing the treacherous mountain cliffs, or crossing narrow boulder strewn tidal beaches.

Early one August spring morning a young lady, Selena Riley, set off for The Patches to hoe the family's first crop of potatoes. After working for an hour or more, she looked up to see the sun rising in the east. It's time for a cup of tea, she thought. Finishing the patch, she walked to the small thatched hut nearby which had a fireplace built in one gable, intending to brew some tea. The hut had no windows, only a low narrow door built at one end. The interior of the hut was very dark.

Selena opened the door to the hut, stooping as she stepped through the door. She put down her bag and squatted before the open fireplace, and began to put wood in place to build a fire. With the wood in place, she turned to rummage in her bag and pulled out a bottle of water, half of which she poured into an empty kettle near the fireside. As she was about to put the kettle onto the unlit fire, she suddenly heard a feeble raspy voice saying, "Could I have a piece of bread and water please?"

Selena almost jumped out of her skin with fright, for on the way to The Patches at Second Watron, she had not seen another person. Second Watron is the furthest site of patches from the village. Trembling, she turned and peered into the furthest corner of the hut, but could not see anything only the dark shadows. "Who's there?" she called in a small voice. There was no answer, only silence, broken by a chesty cough and an insane giggle. The voice then said more strongly, "Give me bread and water!" followed by a low chuckle. This was too much for Selena. She dropped the kettle and rushed out of the hut and ran the three and a half miles back to the village, where, out of breath, she told her story to her family. Dick Riley set off with some other men to the hut at Second Watron, the women following a good distance behind. The men reached the hut and went inside, lighting a candle. They saw a white face of a shivering man, covered by some old sacks.

"Who are you?" Dick asked, as they picked the man up and carried him outside the hut, but the man had passed out. They put him on a donkey and brought him back to the village. Riley took him to his house and they put him to bed. When he started to come round he asked for water. They gave him tea and fed him with some broth. They found out that he was a sailor from a ship that had been wrecked on the south side of the island; the survivors were still there. He had tried to reach the village to get help by climbing over the mountain, after going without food for almost two weeks and only having water to drink, he finally made it to The Patches where he saw the hut and crawled inside, weak from hunger and tormented by thirst. He had suffered memory loss and was not aware he had asked Selena for bread and water.

The next day the islanders launched their boats and sailed to Stony Beach where they found the rest of the crew eating penguins to survive. They brought them back to the settlement where they were reunited with their shipmate, who nearly died trying to get help for them.

FIRESIDE VISITOR

In the late 1800s, during the winter months of June and July, the men of Tristan, when not fishing, would gather up kelp that was washed up on the beaches near the patches to put on a compost heap, for use that coming spring to plant potatoes. Samuel Johnson, a Dane from one of the whaling ships that called at Tristan, had met and married William

Glass's eldest daughter. He settled on Tristan and soon learned how to fend for his family.

William Glass, a deeply religious man of Presbyterian upbringing, had instilled in the other members of the community that no one was to work on a Sunday. All adhered to this, for not wanting to fall out of favour with Glass. Johnson was no exception and had soon also learned 'the early bird catches the worm', whether it would be dung dropped by cattle or kelp washed on to the beach. Late one Saturday, Johnson and some other men had seen several bundles of kelp washed on to the beach near Below The Hill. All had planned to make an early start on Monday morning to collect it for their compost heaps. Johnson, not saying anything to the others went out late Sunday evening. He was going to spend most of the night in a small thatched hut at Below The Hill near the cliffs of boat harbour bay. He planned to start collecting kelp from the beach around ten thirty that night when there would be a full moon.

On reaching the hut, Johnson slung up his hammock, laid several logs in the fireplace, lit his candle and soon had a good fire burning because there was quite a chilly wind blowing from the sea. Before long, he was stretched out in his hammock, dozing before the blazing fire, waiting for the moon to come up over the mountain. As he lay there half asleep, he heard what sounded like something or someone dragging a chain over the stones of the gable. Suddenly there was a mighty puff of wind that came down the chimney and blew out the fire, spreading ashes over the floor. Putting it down to a gust of wind, Johnson got up and poked the fire, put on a few more logs and again had the fire blazing away, setting back in to his hammock.

After a few moments the same thing occurred, but this time Johnson was wide awake. There was no mistaking the clanking of chains on stone; again the fire went out, blown by a gust of wind. This time Johnson got up. The hairs were starting to stand up at the back of his head. He again lit the fire and his candle. Putting it into its holder, he went outside to look around. He did not see anything, although the moon was just rising over the top of Goat Ridge. Going back into the hut he secured the door firmly and again, settled back into the hammock.

No sooner than he was settled, he heard the clanking again. This time the door to the hut flew open and a rush of wind seemed to fill the hut along with the clanking noise. Something brushed against the hammock and blew the fire out and the candle, still in the protection of its glass holder. The door slammed shut again, and then there was silence. This time Johnson was frightened. Like most sailors he was very superstitious and thought this might be because he was going to work on a Sunday. He got out of the hammock and decided to go back home.

By now, the moon had risen, casting long shadows over the small hillocks near the hut. As he left the hut, Johnson heard the clanking noise again, looking over his shoulder he saw a white ghostly apparition coming towards him, about 10 metres away. As fright turned to fear, he ran for his life, back to the village. All the way home Johnson could hear the clanking behind him, getting forever closer. As he neared Jenny's Watron, he felt that that was how far the ghost would come, for he had been told that a spirit never crosses a stream. Well, he was wrong, so very wrong. When he leapt the stream, the ghost leapt right beside him, out of the corner of his eye he saw again the white apparition, and heard the clank of chains. This spurned him to run even faster.

As Johnson reached the gully called 'Joe's Hollow' a few yards from Hottentot Gulch, the ghost appeared to turn up the gully towards the mountain. Moments later, he was at Glass's house hammering at the door. Glass opened the door to find Johnson foaming from the mouth; he was so out of breath. He collapsed in the doorway. The family carried him inside and wrapped him in a warm blanket. That night they could not get anything out of him, only that something blew out the fire.

It was about a month later that he came to his senses, enough to tell them the tale of his fireside visitor.

COME DOWN, MY CHILDREN

During a rather bleak year on Tristan in the late 1800s, most of the men were away from the island. They had gone to Inaccessible to hunt for seals. Only Dick Riley and a few old men were left with the women to tend the sheep and cattle in the village. A sail was sighted approaching the shore. It turned out to be a three-masted schooner from South America. As soon as the ship was anchored, Dick Riley, Old Cotton and some young boys launched a boat and went on board.

The captain, who said he wished to purchase fresh water and some meat, greeted them. Riley and Cotton, being 'old salts', knew there was something strange about the ship. The crew seemed rather sullen and shifty when they tried to barter with them, and they were not allowed below decks. There was a funny smell about the deck. The Captain asked if he could lower a boat to get the fresh water. He was told that he might, so Riley hurriedly got the islanders into their own boats, telling the Captain that he would arrange to get some sheep for them. Once in the boat, Cotton confirmed what Riley already knew, that the ship they had just left was a slaver and the odd smell on the deck was the slaves chained below.

Once ashore, Riley informed the rest of the community about the ship. They caught about two dozen sheep and took them down to the ship's boat on the beach. The sailors from the ship were just finished loading the water barrels into the boats. While the Captain and first mate paid the islanders with sacks of flour, coffee and salt, they enquired where the rest of the men were. Cotton quickly told them that they were on the mountain collecting birds' eggs. The Captain and the mate exchanged knowing looks and the Captain said he was told by a child that the men were gone off in one of the boats to Inaccessible. Riley replied that they would return that day.

The Captain said no more, but he and his mate returned to the ship with the last boat. Unknown to them, Cotton had overheard them discussing the possibility of taking some of the islanders with dark skin as slaves, to replace the slaves they had lost on the long voyage from Africa. That night the elders of the community put their children into the lofts. They were given knives to cut their way out of the thatched roofs and run off into the bushes if the sailors came ashore to capture the islanders. The elders kept watch all night with guns and clubs.

During the night, the wind blew up from the north-east bringing a heavy swell. As it was just breaking first light, the ship weighed anchor and ran before the coming storm. She passed so close to Herald Point that the watchers on the cliff could hear the crew talking to one another. The islanders were most relieved to see the ship sail away. One mother, Martha Green, was so beside herself with relief that she ran to the house in which the children had been hiding, and shouted up into the loft, "Come down my children, come down, you are safe. The ship has now gone!"

LOST WITH ALL HANDS

The 28th November 1885 was going to be a day that was to be remembered by all Tristanians in its short history. For on this fateful day, 15 able-bodied men out of a small community of 18 were lost at sea, leaving behind an island of widows, old men and small children and several youths. Many accounts have been told of the men lost at sea in a new lifeboat while trying to reach a passing ship. This is the islander's version of what took place.

Early that morning just after daybreak there was a shout of "Sail ho!" A sail could be seen passing several miles offshore from the west. Although the wind was blowing from the south-west, about 20 knots, the sea was quite calm. The island men quickly gathered what they needed for trade, launched their new lifeboat and hoisted sail, setting a course to intercept the passing ship. There were 15 able bodied men to crew the boat. It was later learned that the ship was the iron sailing barque, *West Riding*, bound from Bristol to Sydney, under the command of Capt. William Thomas. About two and a half miles off shore, the ship appeared to hove to, and the boat was observed going alongside. It looked to the people watching that the men boarded the ship. A short time later, the barque made sail and stood in towards the east, towing the lifeboat behind her.

Watching from one thousand feet up on Big Point was Sam Swain, with a few boys, with people watching from the cliff at Big Beach. They saw the ship disappear beyond the headland of Big Point. No one was really concerned as they thought that the ship would let the boat off in the lee, as it would be calmer for the men to row back to Big Beach. No one was unduly concerned when the boat failed to show up that day because it was not uncommon for a boat to return the next day from such a venture.

When the boat failed to appear the next day, two parties of men were sent off around the island in both directions, but they soon returned empty handed having seen nothing of the boat and its crew. The community feared the worst: that the boat had either capsized, or drifted out to sea. However, this they did not believe possible, for it meant nothing to the men to row 20 miles to Nightingale or Inaccessible on a day trip. After all, the boat they were using was a new lifeboat built to withstand the rough seas.

What if the men had been forced to stay aboard the ship against their will? But why should they? These were some of the thoughts that crossed the islanders' minds, hoping that this may have been so. The men in the lifeboat had the reputation of being strong, raw-boned and quite hefty in build. None more so than Thomas Glass, would was said to be a handsome man, very strong, and having the build of a Greek god. If backed into a corner in hand-to-hand combat or using cutlasses, it would take two men or more to bring him down. But for those waiting at home, no truth was ever forthcoming. Only it seems, speculation that the boat had capsized, drowning all its occupants.

Two later sceptical reports revealed that one of the islanders in Cape Town had requested the services of a spiritualist, who told them that men were taken aboard the *West Riding* to a far off place, where they were working like slaves. The other was that the Captain of the *West Riding* had hatched a plan with the resident clergyman, Rev. Edwin Dodgson (who favoured removal of the population from the island) to force the men to remain on the ship, so the rest of the community would not survive without their help and would have to leave Tristan. The men from the lifeboat were secretly landed in Saldanha Bay in

South Africa, so the story went. Rev. Dodgson had tried several times to get the people to leave Tristan, even going as far as writing to the British Government about it.

One thing that came to light several years after this tragic incident: while Andrew Swain, who had been a young boy in his late teens when the 15 men were lost, was on board another ship that had called at Tristan to barter goods, he was approached by a sailor who asked him: "Have you got any tassel mats like those I got from the other boat?" "What boat?" Andrew enquired, knowing very well the last boat to have tassel mats to barter, were those taken by the crew of the lost lifeboat. [*A tassel mat is made from the skin of penguins that have been killed for the tassels that grow on their head*].

"The men I got them from was in a lifeboat. That was some years ago," the sailor replied. "That's just what I wanted to know," said Andrew. Suddenly it seemed to dawn on the man what Andrew had said, for he turned and hurried away, disappearing into the hold of the ship, ignoring Andrew, who called to him to come back. Although Andrew made inquiries to find the sailor, no one seemed to know where he was, so even today the story still remains a mystery.

On 28th November 1985, a hundred years later, a plaque was erected in their memory at St Mary's Church on Tristan. A special service was held to commemorate it. Almost all of the island men were at the service, as they felt it was befitting to honour their ancestors' memory.

The plaque reads: -

They have no island graves.
Fifteen men lost without trace 28th November 1885
IN MEMORIAM
Joe Beetham
Thomas and Cornelius Cotton
Thomas Glass
John, William and Alfred Green
Jacob, William and Jeremiah Green
Albert, James and William Hagan
Samuel and Thomas Swain.

[This story is very personal for me as Thomas Glass, one of the boat's crew, was my great-great-grandfather.]

WHAT! A LION ON TRISTAN?

A few years after the lifeboat incident, one of the young boys was herding the sheep near The Bluff, when suddenly he heard a roaring up in The Bluff Gulch. At first he thought it was the sea breaking on the beach, but soon realised it was a calm day. Again the noise came. This time the sheep started to run off towards The Patches. The lad followed them. Looking over his shoulder, he saw what he took to be a large cat, standing at the edge of the gulch.

He ran all the way back to the village to tell of what he had seen and heard. At first the villagers would not believe him, but he insisted that he was telling the truth. So the men took a couple of guns and set off down to The Bluff. When they got there, it was getting dark. They scouted the area and found several large paw prints which one of them took to be made by a lion. A little further on they found a sheep that had been killed, and its throat torn out.

Suddenly, they heard the roar of the lion up on the side of the mountain. Because it was almost dark, the men returned home putting several of the families who did not have any men into the houses of those who had them, for protection. The next day they set off again to look for the lion, but all they found was its droppings and paw prints, and another sheep killed. Before dark the next night, they turned all the sheep and cattle into the pens near the village and again, the families stayed two or more to a house.

In the early hours of the morning, the occupants of Betty Cotton's house were woken up by the bleating of the sheep. Peering through the shuttered windows, they saw a lion with a short length of chain attached to its neck, the end just hitting on the pavement as it walked. The men in the house opened the door slightly and poked their gun through to try and get a shot. As they were about to fire, the lion turned and leapt for the door. Firing the gun at the same time as the lion leapt, the men had just time to shut the door and bar it before the lion struck it with considerable force, shaking the door posts.

For about half an hour it circled the house, and then it moved away. It was full daylight before the people emerged from the house. They related their story to the others. All the women and children were kept in the village for the day as the men and older boys set out to hunt the beast, but they searched the village and Patches area but did not find the lion. All they found were traces of blood in the yard where the lion had been shot. A missing leg of pork that had been hung to cure in one of the outbuildings had been unjointed as if done by a butcher.

The days, weeks, and months passed, nothing was seen or heard of the lion. The islanders deduced it must have come ashore from a wrecked ship and when they shot it they must have wounded it badly and it went off and died somewhere. In fact, almost a year later its skeleton was found at the rocks on the Cave Point, the chain still attached to it.

JACK O' LANTERN OR WILL O'WISP

One day in late spring, my grandfather Jack Rogers (whom I never knew) was up on the mountain collecting birds' eggs with some other men. It had been a fine day to begin with, but the cloud came down later and it got quite misty. Not having watches and knowing that it would get dark soon, they made their way back towards the base above the village.

By the time they reached there it was completely dark and they had to feel their way along the path. Suddenly one of the men said, "Look, there's someone coming to look for us with a light." As they got nearer to the light it started to move away from them. They shouted but got no reply. So they still continued to follow the light, which seemed to be now waiting just ahead of them. As they drew nearer the light suddenly went out. The dogs, which were running ahead, suddenly stopped. When told to move they did not obey, but stood still.

One of the men struck a light and for a moment in the glare of the match, they saw they were standing at the edge of a steep cliff, at the top of Hottentot Gulch. If it had not been for the dogs they would have followed the light and walked over the cliff to fall to certain death, hundreds of feet below. They then realised it was the fabled Jack o' Lantern that had been almost the cause of a dreadful accident.

They scrambled back onto the path, finding their way by following the white tip on the dogs' tails. On reaching the village, they told their story to the other people, who told them no one had been up the mountain to search for them. This was not the last time the other islanders encountered the sinister light, known as Jack o' Lantern. It was especially noticeable on misty nights near the village.

WILD DOG OR SEA MONSTER

One weekend just after the islanders had returned from England in 1963, several of the island men had walked to Stony Beach to earmark some calves. They were staying the night at one of the small huts they had built there. It was dark, about nine o'clock. The men had a fire lit in the hut, and they were settling in for the night, when suddenly the dogs started to bark. Some of them jumped on to the roof of the hut. As they opened the door, the dogs rushed in.

Looking outside they saw what looked like some animal; it was similar in size to a donkey. One of the men threw the door open to go outside to see what it was, when the creature leapt towards the hut. The men quickly shut the door. Looking out again the creature had gone and the dogs seemed to have got over their fright. Next morning when the men checked, they did not find anything to identify this night visitor.

A few months later another group of men saw a similar creature. The dogs again, became frightened. When the men sent the dogs to chase this creature they jumped up barking behind the men. When they went outside they saw the creature moving off into the night up into Stony Beach Gulch. Next morning, when they checked again, they found no tracks or signs of the creature although some men swore they heard what sounded like barking up in Stony Beach Gulch... but then, no one shall ever know what it was they saw.

CHASED BY A WHALE!

On a sunny day one October with the wind light from the south, four men from the Glass family took their 18-foot canvas dinghy to collect driftwood that was washed onto the beach to use as firewood. The men were my uncles Sidney, Godfrey, Wilson and Clement Glass. Making an early start, they rowed the dinghy down to Halfway Beach, so called because it is situated midway between Big Beach and Sandy Point.

After landing the dinghy on the narrow stretch of boulder-strewn beach, they spent an hour or more collecting wood from the sides of the cliff until they had enough wood to load the dinghy. Pulling it down to the edge of the water, they placed a few pieces of stout wood under the keel so it would be easier to launch the dinghy. Half an hour later, with the dinghy loaded to the gunwales, they had the sail hoisted and were heading back to the village. Sidney was at the helm as they sailed slowly along, while the others relaxed, enjoying a smoke. As they neared Jew's Point, Godfrey suddenly pointed and said, "Look, there's a whale."

They all turned to look just in time to see a sperm whale dive under water about one hundred yards astern of the dinghy. "That whale seem to be on its own," Clement remarked, but no one took much notice of this, as they were now quite used to seeing whales about this time of year. Moments later there was a mighty splash, as the whale surfaced under the dinghy, almost capsizing it. The men were caught by surprise. Sidney was thrown off the stern into the sea along with the rudder and a few bundles of wood that were packed there. The other men quickly lowered the sail and looked around for Sidney, who was nowhere to be seen.

Sidney, when he was thrown from the dinghy, landed on the whale's back. The whale, feeling the weight of Sidney on his back dived under taking Sidney with him. Down, down, down they went, the water changing to a darker blue the deeper they went. Suddenly Sidney was free. With his lungs bursting he kicked out for the surface, he broke the surface several yards from the dinghy. He could hear the others shouting, but it was a few seconds before he could understand them. Then he was aware of Godfrey shouting, "Grab hold of the rope, brother, and we will pull you in."

Godfrey then threw the rope and Sidney held on as Godfrey pulled him into the safety of the dinghy. Meanwhile Clement and Wilson had got out the oars to keep the dinghy steady. They pulled Sidney into the dinghy with his clothes torn in several places, his legs and body cut and bleeding quite badly.

With Sidney in the boat, Clement and Wilson started to row for the shore at Jew's Point. Godfrey shouted then: "Look, the whale's chasing the boat." Clement and Wilson rowed with all their strength to reach the beach. Godfrey grabbed an extra oar to help them row. Sidney although still bleeding, put on a steering oar to keep the dinghy straight. Pulling strongly at the oars, they reached the beach. About five minutes later the whale was still following a few yards behind them.

Luckily it was flat calm when they reached the beach. Usually there would be surf breaking on the beach. Without breaking stroke, they grounded the dinghy, pulling it onto the beach. Wilson and Clement jumped out, thigh deep into the water grabbing hold of the dinghy so it would not slew sideways onto the beach, while Godfrey relieved Sidney at the steering oar helping to keep the stern steady.

The whale stopped a few yards from the dinghy, unable to come any closer as the water was too shallow. With a trumpet-like whoosh, the whale blew a torrent of water into the air, and dived under the water. As the men watched, the whale headed out to the spot where it had hit the dinghy. When the whale reached where the wood was floating, it started jumping out of the water, smacking its tail into the water, and throwing the rudder and bits of wood into the air.

The men from the beach watched in amazement, as they had never seen anything like that happen in their entire life. The whale continued to leap about in the same area smashing the wood to bits with mighty whacks of its tail. On shore, Sidney bandaged his cuts on his legs with strips of cloth torn from his shirt. Ten minutes later the whale dived for the last time, not to reappear again. Taking no chances, the men waited another ten minutes before backing the dinghy into the sea, and rowing the last mile to Big Beach, keeping about five yards from the shore and a wary eye open in case the whale reappeared.

Reaching Big Beach without further incident, Sidney went home to get his leg properly dressed, while the others unloaded the wood from the dinghy. On the way from the beach, Sidney met his father, Robert Glass, and told him of the incident. Robert, known as Bob, chuckled when he heard what had happened, for he had spent many years of his life working on the whaling ships out of New Bedford, where he obtained the rank of Second Mate and Sailing Master.

He had told his sons that a whale did not attack boats unless it was provoked. Sidney walked off indignantly knowing that he would not believe another of his father's tales about his days on the whaling ships!

THE HURRICANE THAT STRUCK TRISTAN IN 2001

Sunday 20th May, 2001, was a sunny day. The wind was very light, blowing from the south east. Although it was early winter on Tristan, one would not have believed so. It was like a summer day. Several of the island men were planning to go out fishing in the boats the next day.

A week or so earlier, we had a very bad storm from the south west with gale force winds. It blew off part of the roof of Harold Green's house, and blew down a huge pine tree, known by the islanders as the 'Christmas Tree' that grew out near The Patches at the foot of the mountain known locally as 'The Wash'. This was only a taste of what was to come. After midnight onwards, the wind started to increase, but being Tristan, no one took any notice of this. By first light, the wind was blowing at gale force, still from the south east, and it was pouring with rain. I was woken at seven o'clock by a banging on the roof of my house. I found it was caused by the asbestos bargeboard on the east gable of the house. I shouted to my son Leon and we quickly put on waterproofs and shouted to Warren and my father next door to help us nail back the bargeboard. Because we did not have the proper asbestos screws, we used five inch nails instead. While my father cut rubber from an old fishing buoy, I drilled holes in the asbestos. Warren and Leon nailed down the bargeboard. We had to hold on to each other during the strongest gusts of wind.

As soon as we had finished, Leon and I went to see if everything was alright at his grandmother's house. After checking the house, we found everything intact. Catherine was rather alarmed as the roof had blown off the east slaughter house, which is only several metres from her home. I assured her all was well and told her one of us would pop back later to check on things, as she was living on her own. Leon and I returned home, got his Jeep and left for work. All the school children were taken to school by their parents. By 09.30 the wind had increased in ferocity, gusting to about 75 knots or more.

At the Administration building, the door had to be secured by a large bolt from inside to prevent it being blown open. Anyone wishing to leave or enter the building had to be let in or out by a member of the staff. The wind blew the rain through the windows and the roof was leaking. The floor was covered in places with water. James Glass (who was the Acting Administrator at the time) and I watched the scene outside from his office window, as the men in green and red waterproofs struggled against the wind as they set about their tasks.

The men from the factory had just returned from securing the fishing boats in the harbour around the factory buildings. Benny Green (Assistant Factory Manager), had let them off work, as there were reports of damage to houses in the village. During this time as we looked on, parts of the zinc and asbestos roofs belonging to the gas store, PWD (Public Works Department) garage, supermarket and agriculture store were blown away. Meanwhile, the men from the Government workforce were directed by the Heads of Department to try to secure the damaged buildings as best as they could.

As the reports of buildings being damaged drifted in, I asked James if he would like me to go and speak to each Head of Department for him and report back. That way he would be better informed about what was happening. He agreed, so I headed out into the storm which was so bad now that I had to shelter from the worst gusts of wind.

After speaking to each Head of Department and getting a damage report, I headed to the school to find all the teachers and pupils gathered in the school hall as the PVC guttering had blown off and part of the roof was starting to lift as well. Anne Green (who was Acting Headmistress at the time as the Headmistress, Marlene, was away on a training course) was on the point of closing the school and sending out word for parents to collect their children. The school can be a very dangerous place when a gale is on, as it has many windows and teachers are always concerned that if something blows and hits the windows with the pupils inside, the consequences could be drastic.

I left the school to ask Karl Hagan (Head of PWD) to send some men to secure the roof of the school, passing word on to any parents to collect their children. At about 10.30, half an hour after leaving the Government Building, I reported back to James Glass, who made an immediate decision to close down the work for the day, so people could secure their homes against further damage. I left to pass on the word and to evacuate the school. The last group of about 12 teachers and pupils were collected by Joe Green and Trevor Glass in their Land Rover and pick-up truck. Trevor dropped my wife Sharon (a teacher at the school) at our house. By now some of the overhead electrical cables had blown off their poles.

We had just got into the house when Jack appeared shouting that the roof of my father's house was starting to lift. We grabbed hammers and the nails that I had bought from the PWD in case of such an event and rushed to nail the asbestos down. While Warren and I re-nailed the roof, Jack and my Father packed stones and bricks onto the flat part to it to weigh it down.

We had just finished when Warren shouted, "Look out!" I glanced up to see pieces of fibreglass from the roof of the vestry on the Anglican Church flying through the air towards us. We ducked out of the way grabbing them as they came up against the wall and weighed them down with stones to prevent our windows being broken. As I looked up, I saw Neil Swain whose house is just below ours, crawling on his hands and knees on to the top of his roof, holding on for dear life, while trying to push a couple of bricks in front of him to weigh down the flat roof of his house.

I pointed to Neil's' dilemma and the others rushed off to help him. I finished knocking the last few nails into the asbestos roofing on my father's house and went to help them. Jack was passing up the bricks to Neil while Warren, who had just joined him on his roof, held onto him as he placed the bricks. Once the bricks were in place, they put a couple of ropes over the roof and secured them to the ground.

Neil said he was helping his father-in-law Peter Repetto to secure his roof, when he received word that the asbestos on his house was starting to lift and only got back in time to secure it. This was the scene throughout the village as neighbours rushed to help each other, only to be called back to their own homes to prevent the roofs from being blown off. Jack, Warren and I finished checking the other buildings and finished by securing our garage doors. Leon, who was at his grandmother's house during this time, returned to say that Aron Swain's roof had just blown off and pieces of asbestos had hit Donald Hagan's roof, breaking the asbestos and Donald's roof had also blown off. Also the roof of the Community Centre was starting to break off and blow away. Several sheets of asbestos had been blown off Joe Green's roof at the rear of the house.

By now the wind was really strong. Checking the time I saw that it was 13.30. Since leaving work, almost two hours had passed and we had only been into my fathers' house for about 10 minutes for a cup of tea. I left immediately for Catherine's house, taking the Jeep, fearing asbestos from Joe's house would blow and smash into her home, causing more damage. On the way I saw the ground was strewn with debris. Broken bits of asbestos littered the road, some pieces the size of my hand, others over a metre long about 30 centimetres wide, still with bits of wood fastened to them. Several electrical cables were lying across the road; the roof of the Community Centre was still breaking up.

Catherine's roof and the two houses next door were still intact. They belonged to Sharon's sister Lorraine and her Aunt Gracie. Maybe this was partly because Leon and I had already nailed them with asbestos screws a week before. I decided that it would be best if I stayed down at Catherine's for the rest of the day. That night if there was an accident, I maybe could stop the roof from being destroyed.

I returned home and parked the Jeep in the lee of a high stone wall, informed Leon and Sharon what my plan was. I then gave Leon the hammer and nails in case he needed them, and returned to Catherine's. I checked around the house, secured the radio aerials (belonging to my brother-in-law, who is a radio ham) and settled down to prepare for the worst, with wood, nails, and hardboard, for boarding up a window if it got broken. One could hear the gusts of wind approaching in a screaming crescendo, when they hit the house the whole structure would shake, each time this happened I had visions of the whole house imploding. I ventured out twice more during the evening to nail down some zinc on Alice Glass's potato hut, and remove and secure some PVC guttering and a small chicken coop that had blown to the back of the house.

Sometime after midnight, the wind backed more to the south west and died down, but it was still raining. All the houses on the island were wet due to the rain being driven through the windows and roofs by the wind. By first light, the rain had eased off. People emerged from their homes awestruck and dumbfounded by the sight that greeted them. The village was a mess! The debris from the storm littered about. There were broken pieces of asbestos, wood tree branches, zinc, electric cables lying about the place. It was as if a giant's hand had taken his axe and gone mad, smashing the village to bits.

Tristanians are used to experiencing gales, but not one on the scale of this tempest. But true to their nature, the islanders sorted out their most important issues. First, that was to re-roof the houses that had lost or damaged their roofs. Around 16.00 the previous evening, the east gable and part of the roof of the hospital had blown down, destroying the operating theatre, the X-ray room and part of the Doctor's house. The slates had blown off the roof. Young Patrick Green had been admitted to hospital earlier, so the doctor and his family spent the night at the hospital.

The island men sorted themselves into several groups, each going to different houses to help the unfortunate owner to repair the damage to their roof. Some families only had part of their roof damaged. Within a couple of hours, the broken sheets of asbestos had been replaced. Aron Swain and Donald Hagan's had the worst of the damage. Their roofs took the better part of the day to repair.

The people who had to replace or repair most of their roofs were: Donald Hagan, Aron Swain, Lewis Glass, Derek Rogers, Peter Repetto, Dorothy Rogers, John Elsemore, James Glass' guest house, The Government guest house, the Doctor's house and the Factory guest house. The east bulk store of the Factory was destroyed, the RSJ iron girders twisted and bent like they were made from putty. The Community Centre had lost its roof. The 100 foot radio mast was twisted and bent at the base in shape of the letter S. Several islanders had lost the roofs of their garages and potato huts. St Mary's Anglican Church had the vestry roof blown off. The Government had 20 buildings with part of, or the entire roof, completely damaged.

Three of the longboats that were tied down with rope, had been blown on to the lawn in front of the Administrator's house. *Raffee* and *Britannia* were found lying in the middle of the lawn. *Lorna* was blown across the lawn into the flax garden near the Padre's house, only the bow of the boat could be seen from the Administrator's lawn.

Just after midday, the day following the hurricane, Leon, Jack, Warren, Ches Lavarello and I went out to check the potato patches for damage. I took Andy's Toyota 4x4 as it was still wet off the road. We made a note of 26 camping huts and potato huts which had been destroyed or damaged. The wind was still gusting strongly. Several sheep we saw were blown about like beach balls. We also found a couple of cattle blown over in the ditches. In all, more than 100 sheep and about 30 head of cattle were lost. On returning home, we informed the owners, and went to help Aron and Donald with replacing their damaged roofs.

During the evening of the hurricane, people who had their roofs damaged left their homes to move in with family or friends or neighbours. Several had some hair-raising experiences.

Yvonne Glass (Lewis Glass's wife) said she was standing in her kitchen looking out of the window, when she saw what looked like a small whirlwind coming from the direction of the volcano road, towards their house. Suddenly there was a loud bang, the entire house shook, and she saw two pieces of asbestos blown into the front yard. When Lewis checked the cause of the noise, he found several sheets of asbestos missing from his roof. The family moved to Harold Green's house which was a few metres down the road from Lewis' house, where they spent the night. Lewis said he prayed that there would be no further damage caused to his home, as it was one of the most exposed houses in the village, being built on a hill. He had just finished a major refurbishment of the house. His prayers were answered, for the next morning, apart from the water inside the house, he was able to repair his roof in a few hours. Lewis' house was the only house in the village that was destroyed during the eruption of the volcano in 1961, when a piece of red hot lava set the thatched roof on fire and burnt the house down.

Barney Swain (the head electrician for the fishing factory) was just returning home from switching off the electrical power to the village: with broken electrical cables and water about, he feared someone could otherwise have been electrocuted. He had almost reached his home near the Community Centre, when he had to dive to avoid being hit by a six foot length of three inch steel pipe. Picking himself up, Barney saw that one end of the pipe was embedded firmly into the ground, at the same place that he was previously standing. The pipe was standing upright like a thrown javelin.

Albert Green, who was on his way to the hospital to be with his son Patrick, was suddenly caught by a gust of wind and pushed along the ground as if he was no heavier than a child. Albert, who is nearly six feet tall and very strong, looked up to see a boulder in his path. It took all his strength to roll his body to avoid crashing head first into it.

Over the next week, the men worked to restore the hospital roof, and the roofs of all the other Government buildings that had been destroyed. The women cleaned up the debris throughout the village, as the electricians worked to restore the power supply to homes. It was about a week before the electricity was on line and the children were able to return to school. I worked with the rest of the men to help to restore the damage. All frozen foods were taken from people's refrigerators in their homes to be placed into the factory freezers until the electricity was restored. For a week Tristanians worked to bring things back to normal in the aftermath of the hurricane.

After the news got out, donations of money were received from the UK, South Africa and Falklands and many other places to help Tristan to restore the damage to buildings. This money, along with monthly contributions from all working Tristanians, is put into a special fund called the Disaster Fund, something that had not existed before the hurricane. The Tristanians were most grateful to all who helped by sending money to help the island, and James Glass sent word of thanks back to them on behalf of the island.

A few months later the *Wave Dancer* Patrol Boat, and the *Wave Dancer* RIB went across to Nightingale to see if there was any damage.

They found that 18 of the huts had been destroyed, or damaged. Several could not be re-built on their former sites as it was deduced that if the longboats had been at Nightingale at that time, they would all been destroyed and there would have been the possibility that some people may have been killed or injured in their huts when they were washed away. Since then, many islanders have cleared away sites on top of the cliffs, to build their huts, but as to this day, no huts have been built.

In all, life on Tristan has changed since the hurricane. It is a community policy that all houses in the village must have their asbestos roofs replaced by zinc, which is much stronger and less of a health hazard. This is paid for by the Disaster Fund. One can see the results, as several of the houses have already had their roofs changed.

STAMPS, COINS AND HANDICRAFTS

Tristan da Cunha may be the world's most remote inhabited island, but that makes its postage stamps and its handicrafts of special interest. In recent years, coins specially produced for collectors have proved increasingly popular and their sale makes a real contribution to the economy of our island.

In fact, its postage stamps are some of the most sought after in the world. They are highly prized and tell the story of the island, its people and their unique environment. The evacuation of the island and the return of the islanders after the eruption of the volcano produced some very interesting stamps and some of these, used on envelopes written by returning islanders, have sold at auction for many hundreds of pounds.

The first stamps for Tristan da Cunha were the 1938-49 issues of St. Helena overprinted 'TRISTAN DA CUNHA' in black in the late 1940's. The first stamp issued by Tristan da Cunha on its own was the 1953 Coronation of Queen Elizabeth II commemorative. The postal history and philately of Tristan da Cunha has not surprisingly attracted a very large following of enthusiasts who have their own international society, the St Helena, Ascension, and Tristan da Cunha Philatelic Society, Inc. contactable via webmaster@atlanticislands.org. It organises worldwide auctions and its magazine, the South Atlantic Chronicle, has won awards for its excellence.

One of the designers of the what are known as 'potato stamps' issued in 1946, when postage was paid for with potatoes, Allan B Crawford, wrote about his experiences in his book *Penguins, Potatoes, & Postage Stamps, A Tristan da Cunha Chronicle* (published by Anthony Nelson, ISBN 0-904614-689; mikejcrawford@hotmail.com).

Today, stamp designs include royalty and royal anniversaries, events from the island's history (such as the anniversary of my pioneering ancestor William Glass, to whom a whole miniature sheet was devoted), birds and other wildlife, ships and everyday life on the island. A series devoted to Allan Crawford's life proved popular with collectors, as have more recent issues showing The Potato Patches, the fishing industry, how mail reaches our island, Tristan traditions and seafaring. Our population is so small, you may recognise some of the people you meet on Tristan on our stamps: I'm on the 35p stamps showing mail being delivered to Tristan and I'm on another 35p celebrating island traditions – this time with my border collie Scout, taking part in Ratting Day. Even my Police Land Rover has appeared on a stamp!

New series (which are always produced in association with Casco Philatelic of the UK, after consultation with the Island Council's Stamp Committee) celebrate island surnames, more Tristan traditions and for everyday use, conservation – itself now a major feature of island life, reflecting islanders' care for the wildlife with which they share their lives.

The stamps can be obtained through dealers around the world or through on-line auctions such as e-Bay, but when collectors buy them from the Post Office on Tristan, they make a very direct contribution to the island's economy. It can of course take weeks and occasionally months for orders to be delivered, because of the remoteness of the island, but Iris Green, our Postmistress, does deal with orders sent in from around the world. Orders can be made by open-dated (i.e. undated) cheques drawn on a UK bank, by cash (£ sterling, rands, US $ and Euro notes, which should be sent by registered post), by banker's draft or on a British Postal Order. You can keep up to date with forthcoming issues, covers and collector's items via the joint Tristan Government and Association website, on www.tristandc.com

Collectors can deposit a sum of money at the Tristan Post Office with a note of what they'd like (used or unused stamps, miniature sheets, covers and so on) and a Statement of Account is sent from Tristan with every order. Normally these orders are sent by Registered Post for a small additional charge.

The address of our brand new Post Office and its helpful and efficient team, is quite simply: Iris Green, Postmistress, Edinburgh-of-the-Seven-Seas, Tristan da Cunha, South Atlantic Ocean, TDCU 1ZZ.

Many of the islanders make handicrafts for sale to people visiting from cruise ships or who write in from around the world. Pullovers, cardigans, gloves, socks and bed socks are particularly popular - and so too are some rather winsome if slightly lop eared knitted penguins (large and small) with a Tristan label stitched neatly to their backsides! Items for sale - which includes a small number of souvenirs made abroad specially for the island - can be seen on www.tristandc.com or a list is available by post from The Tristan Souvenir Shop, Edinburgh-of-the-Seven Seas, Tristan da Cunha, South Atlantic Ocean, TDCU 1ZZ. The range is constantly being expanded and improved. Be patient when placing your order or enquiry - it can take some months for correspondence to get backwards and forwards! One purchaser of a Tristan sweater was amused to be told the reason for its late delivery was that the sheep first had to be caught, shorn and then the wool spun, before his order could be fulfilled! The process took two years but it is quicker now and we have a brand new handicrafts shop on the island for visitors and for Tristan islanders selecting gifts for friends.

Coins: while Tristan's stamps are renowned worldwide even among non-collectors, the really big growth has come in the popularity of specially produced souvenir coin sets, which make a very real contribution to our economy, thanks to an agreement with their producer, Commonwealth Mint. You'll not find many (if any) in your small change on the island, as we use UK coins and bank notes. I'd like to see more available for sale to cruise ship passengers and other visitors. It's something we've discussed with the producers. But there's no doubting their popularity. Special issues follow themes popular with collectors (such as historic ships): other sets commemorate wildlife around the island and there are even issues for some of our outlying islands, such as Stoltenhoff. Some of the coins are produced for investors using precious metals such as platinum, gold and silver. You can sometimes find the coins on eBay and in special numismatists' shops. Further details can be had from the producers via http://www.thecommonwealthmint.co.uk or call (from Tristan or UK) 08453 035993; PO Box 1067, Bromley BR1 9QF, UK.

PERSONAL GLIMPSES

As I write this final chapter, I reflect on changes that have affected generations of Tristanians. From that day on 14th August 1816, when my great grandfather of seven generations, William Glass, first set foot on this lonely windswept isle, I feel that he set out to create a lifestyle in which all men are equal, no matter of rank, status or the colour of their skin. Even to this day, the roots of his legacy still stand, although the ideals and lifestyle of the present day Tristanians have changed. Whatever the outcome of our future, I think it's important to retain our identity in which we can rely on the help of our neighbours, no matter what the circumstances.

I have read just about every book written about Tristan. Some are by authors who have never been to the island. Others are by people who only spoke to Tristanians at Calshot in England during the evacuation of 1961. The underlying theme that interests them most is the character and lifestyle of the community. A few of the points I find rather offensive, particularly when reference is made to the islanders' intelligence. The older generation of Tristanians were not country bumpkins, even though they lacked a basic education. During the 1938 Norwegian Expedition to Tristan, the sociologist Peter Munch described the islanders as being 'a new race and a bit lazy'. I beg to differ. Mr Munch only stood on the outside and looked in, like so many others. He never got up before the crack of dawn, toiled a full day at The Patches, spent a day up the mountain gathering wood for the fire or spent a day off fishing with no food to eat until that evening. If he did, he would know this is not the lifestyle that breeds laziness. The moral issue of interbreeding and 'a new race' seems to be one of the points that some visitors appear to seek evidence for. Going back as far as the 1830s, our ancestors came from Europe and South Africa. We are not prodigies of Charles Darwin's missing link who have just fallen out of the trees.

Living in a remote isolated environment for more than a hundred years shapes our customs and way of life. Tristanians as a whole have tenacious views when it comes to their private lives. The simple reason is that they have been subjected to a media that doesn't print the truth about Tristan but cares more about what will increase sales of magazines or books. Some of the missionary priests were not very subtle in their writing about the island. Some treated the islanders like second-class citizens. The Reverend J. Graham Barrow, although maybe not intentionally, started a feud between the Repetto and Glass families for leadership on the island.

That carried on for years. The fact of the matter is that my great grandfather, Robert (Bob) Glass was wise to the ways of the world, having worked for many years on the whaling ships out of New Bedford, reaching the rank of second mate. Then he served with Kitchener's Scouts during the Boer War and after, as foreman of a diamond mine in the Orange Free State. So, he would not be subjected to the whims of a priest on how he should conduct his life. It rather seems then, as it can be today, not what you know, but whom you know, that gets you certain privileges.

This was used to good effect when the Reverend Augustus Partridge was appointed magistrate in 1932. During his years in office he appointed an island council over which he wielded such power that he had two men from the Repetto family whip another from the Swain family with a bullock whip made from a single strip of hide over his naked back until he bled, crying out in pain. Richard Swain had been banned by Reverend Partridge from speaking to or associating with other islanders for a previous 'offence' of allowing his dog to kill sheep: an allegation he denied. Richard Swain chose to disobey and went to The Caves fishing with Cyril Rogers, who was a witness to what had happened. The two men from the Repetto Clan were given this grim task by Partridge holding out a pack of playing cards and the man who drew the highest card would carry out the whipping. The highest card turned out to be ace of clubs. The man who drew the lower card guarded the gate to prevent anyone from entering.

Partridge also had two women put into the stocks outside the church to make a public spectacle of them. One of them was my grandmother,

Rose Rogers (a widow at the time) because her dog was suspected of chasing sheep. So much for human rights, and this was a man of God – or supposed to be! More like a tyrant! It makes me angry to think of it, even all these years after she told me about the incident. One thing is for sure: no one else ever tried to exact such measures on the Glass clan.

On the whole Tristanians are no different than people from other parts of the world. As in any small village, gossip is rife and there is a tendency to keep up with the Jones. People in the community are not of a violent nature. As in the past, it is the trend to always help people in trouble or less fortunate than themselves. This I believe stems from the norms passed down by our forefathers who time after time, risked their lives and who took in and fed sailors from over a dozen or more wrecked ships. Even though at times they were near to starving, they never lured passing ships onto the rocks by lighting false beacons.

Tristanians are a religious community and any twist of fate is referred to as the 'Will of God'.

Many people believe that Tristanians lack the motive or will to accept the responsibility of leadership when organising community projects and have to look to expatriates for guidance. Well, they should observe island men roofing an islander's private house; unloading, loading or pulling the longboats on to the rock at Nightingale; slaughtering several cattle at The Caves or Stony Beach.

There is an unwritten code. Each member of the group fits into the role like cogs in a well-oiled machine. The more experienced men will take the responsibility of directing the others. However for Government projects, it doesn't work that way. Because there are differences in the rank and status, one man is the supervisor, the others the work force. The supervisor has the material knowledge, but has not had the managerial training that is needed for leadership in an economic industry.

The people of Tristan have survived on the island over the years, due to their beliefs in themselves and the Will of God to overcome the many arduous tasks that have come their way.

When a former Administrator, Brian Baldwin, asked the Island Council to come up with a motto describing the Tristanians, to put on the Tristan flag, I came up with the idea (having read about the history of Tristan) that the motto should be: 'Our Faith is our Strength'. The Council accepted this and it was put on the Tristan da Cunha coat of arms. I feel that this is why the islanders are still living on Tristan today. James Glass drew the design for the crest, and largely due to his efforts, we now have the flag of Tristan flying over the village.

Life has changed on Tristan from 1961 up to the present day. The attitudes of the people have also changed. People are becoming more individual and materialistic in their way of life, putting more precedence into the value of money, than growing potatoes. I feel that now money is just as important to them, as their potatoes, sheep and cattle. We cannot do more of one or less of the other, if we want to keep enjoying the standard of our present lifestyle. It seems some of the younger generation are not so industrious as their peers, when it comes to tending their potato patches.

One of the vices of the outside world that has had a bit of a down side on Tristan was the importation of alcohol. Like smoking tobacco, alcohol over a period of time creates its own problems. In the UK, it is binge drinking that causes anti-social behaviour. On Tristan, it is the casual acceptance of alcohol as part of the way of life. In any society, the youth of today will follow a similar lifestyle to their peers. There are mostly a minority of individuals who can create problems for others.

As a police officer, I have sometimes been criticized for doing my job, either being too firm handed, or too lax in applying the law - but at the same time, no one is willing to step into my shoes. I have always tried to conduct myself as professionally as possible using a tactful, firm but fair approach to each problem. Maybe at times I was too diplomatic in my dealings with people. It's not an easy thing to do, policing a community in which people are related through birth or marriage. As the only police officer, my family have often been ostracised and had to bear the brunt of opprobrium for my actions. After all, I have to try to police the community in such a way that the law is upheld and that I am still accepted as a member of the community.

I feel that I have improved in my work and learned from any mistakes I have made. When several people initially asked me to stand for election as Chief Islander (Head Councillor), having previously held the post of Deputy President of the Island Council, I felt it would not be right to accept such a position because of plans to go on leave for six months, and to take another six months as a working holiday.

I first joined the police force at St Helena in April 1986 where I spent a year working, and returned to Tristan in February 1987 to be appointed as a part time constable. When Sergeant Albert Glass retired in 1989, I took over running the police, still part time, until I went to England in November 1992 with my family for a year. I trained with the Hertfordshire Constabulary, doing ten weeks at Shotley Police College in Suffolk on basic training; then I attended specialised courses in North Hertfordshire with traffic, CID, scenes of crime, domestic violence, alcohol abuse, town centre beat and rural patrol with the village police officers. In addition, I trained with customs and immigration at Luton Airport. I enjoyed my time policing with Hertfordshire Constabulary. I made many good friends among the police; a particular friend was, and still is, is Alan Bruce who's from Scotland. We became the best of friends soon after I returned from Shotley.

I returned to Tristan in September 1993 and was promoted to Sergeant, and took over running the police. Search and rescue were soon added to my list of responsibilities and customs, immigration and conservation had been part of the police responsibilities. Later on, I got involved with the cruise ships. I was awarded a commendation in 1997 and promoted to Inspector in January 1998. I travelled to the UK again in December 1998 to carry out a 12 -week police refresher course in North Hertfordshire Police. It was great to see Alan again. During our off duty hours we had some good times, visiting the highlights of London. I also did another stint at Luton Airport; then a week at Bangor in Wales on a mountain rescue management course, moving on to Salcombe in Devon on a coxswains' course for driving RIB (Rigid Inflatable Boats) in which I passed two RYA (Royal Yacht Association) coxswains' certificates, standard and advanced. I returned to Tristan in June 1999.

From all my police training, I have learned a lot when dealing with people from all walks of life. It does make me angry when I see people who come to Tristan from other countries try to take advantage of Tristanians because they think they are wiser to the ways of the world than the islanders.

A classic example was when an Administrator who, having finished his term of office, became a managing director of a company that had major investments in Tristan's economy. It seemed as if this person used this to further his own career. There is a general opinion on Tristan that this led to decades of the company exploiting the people of the island. It's safe to say the present company that has replaced the old one seems sincere in its dealings with Tristan. Not only have they contributed to the welfare of the island by increasing the standard of the present lifestyle, their employees have benefited as well.

This I feel has come about as the people of Tristan are better educated and more forthright in their dealings with people from England and South Africa and that has created a relationship in which respect is earned on both sides.

But there are still those who visit Tristan and believe they are above the laws on the island and conduct themselves as though they were lords of the manor, while treating Tristanians as third world citizens. In my office as Inspector of Police and during my time as Deputy President of the Island Council, I had some altercations with such people who made verbal threats to destroy my welfare just because I stood up for what I thought was right for the island. During a written exchange of confidential issues concerning the Island Council, this same person demanded I reveal verbal information to them. My answer to that was to say, "Correct me if I'm wrong, but we live in a democracy with the right to speak and express our beliefs, without being subjected to the Hitler syndrome."

I have certain beliefs that have served me well during my time in office as a police officer and councillor and I was not about to compromise them because of a lot of political jargon or verbal paraphernalia.

At times I have had the feeling that sometimes Tristan has had the rotten end of the stick when people from overseas have been chosen to help us run our island. In darker moments, I've wondered whether we should design our own recruitment slogan: 'Welcome to Tristan da Cunha, the island that's left to fend on its own'.

After returning home in 1998, I ran a youth group for ages nine to 15 during my spare time. While at a Youth and School Liaison meeting at Letchworth in Hertfordshire, I read a quote that was pinned to one of

the walls of the building where the meeting was held. It read:
> *Do not teach boys to train by force and harshness! But lead them by what amuses them so they may better understand the bent of their minds.*   PLATO

This quote would explain some people's beliefs that actions are louder than words. Of all the authors who have written books about Tristan, I feel that the most honest account comes from Mrs Rose Rogers in *The Lonely Island*, and by Allan Crawford: *I Went to Tristan da Cunha*.

Yes, Tristan da Cunha: where people can sleep without locking their doors at night, knowing they won't be burgled and where children can play without the fear of being molested.

Yes, Tristan: its community protected by the vast waters of the Atlantic from the everyday evils of the world.

Tristan has changed more over the past 50 years since the 1961 volcanic eruption, than in all its past history. Money has the most effect on how we live today. The fishing industry has improved over the last two decades, thanks to James Glass, who played an important part in its management. James is one of the four islanders who have held the post of Acting Administrator. The other three are his sister Anne Green, Lewis Glass MBE and subsequently, I have carried out the duty for two periods.

Twenty years ago young couples getting married usually built an extension on to their parents' houses, then added more extensions over the years. Now, young couples can build a new complete house out of concrete and have them fully furnished when they are married. Most houses on the island have fitted kitchen units and ceramic tiled floors.

Tristan now has its own property in Cape Town: a house with a garage and four flats. Many people have been on holiday there and for medical treatment. Eugene and Joy Stoffberg are the managers for the property: Joy was born on Tristan and Eugene is well known and liked as a retired skipper familiar with the perils of Tristan waters.

The first major input into island life was electricity, which was installed and switched on, on 25th September 1969. Paraffin stoves replaced the wood fires; gas stoves in turn replaced them. Gas water heaters now replaced the wood fuelled water heaters. People imported domestic box freezers and fridges.

Hi-fi stereo systems replaced record players and transistor radios, television and video recorders replaced the weekly films shown at the community centre. Soon, with a public video library on offer, people did not go to the pub so much. Every home on the island has a TV screen and a video/DVD player. A small café was also opened for service on late afternoons and weekends. A new hospital and school were built in the late 1960s and early 1970s, though both are now in need of updating. A swimming pool was built next to the site of the original café, now enabling all children in school to learn to swim. The 1980s saw the importance emerging of motorbikes and scooters.

Music was taught at the school and a few local bands were formed. Guitars, drums and keyboards: a far cry from the original Tristan dances, for which the music was supplied by the fiddle and accordion. Islanders started to build camping huts out at The Patches, where they spent weekends and Christmas holidays. Satellite TV replaced the video library in 2001. People on Tristan can now see the BBC News live and a good coverage of the sports and British soaps - and the youngest children joined the millions round the world who watch the *Teletubbies*.

Most families would celebrate the Christmas holidays together, by two families joining up together and living at one of their houses for the two weeks. This no longer happens. They will often go out for a day to have a barbecue or 'braai' as the Tristanians call it.

In the 1990s, people brought in pick-ups, Land Rovers and cars for private use. They no longer depended on Government transport, which were the tractors, to bring the crop of potatoes home from The Patches. The roads have been improved. The last bullock carts were used for a brief period in the early 1980s.

From 1985, islanders were replacing the Heads of Government Departments who used to be expatriates, though some outsiders have more recently been hired in to give extra support. The Administrator is both Magistrate and President of the Island Council. He's appointed by the Foreign Office in London. The Public Works Department is being managed by South African Henning Myburgh (who's accompanied on the island by his wife Linda). A popular former head teacher, Jim Kerr, is back on the island as Education Advisor, helping with teacher training and beefing up the curriculum so that the school leaving age can be raised to 16 and with an eye to better prospects for island pupils wanting to go on to higher education. He too is accompanied by his wife, Sue.

Nicare, an organisation described as 'an arm of the personal health and social services in Northern Ireland' which has carried out work in health, social care and social security in over 40 developing countries in the last decade, appoints the Doctor, (our current doctor is a surgeon from India, Dr Nagarajan Sridhar) There are now sometimes two clergymen looking after the congregations of the Anglican and Catholic churches. The Anglicans are the largest denomination: their church is called St Mary's - the Catholic church is called St Joseph's. The whole community helped to build both churches. At the time of editing, both churches were again without incumbents.

The Government is split into several departments, each with its own responsibilities.

ADMINISTRATION is the responsibility of HM Administrator (an employee of the UK Government's Foreign and Commonwealth Office), who is in charge of the smooth running of the infrastructure and ultimately, of all the Government departments and responsible to London. The Administrator's 'line manager' is the Governor on St. Helena, who also has responsibility for Ascension Island. Tristan does not have its own Governor. Since changes in 2009 which meant that Tristan and Ascension were no longer dependencies of St. Helena, the system is best described as one territory (St. Helena, Tristan and Ascension), with three governments - one for each of the very distinctive and widely separated islands.

AGRICULTURE, under Neil Swain, is responsible for sheep, cattle, grazing land and veterinary work. It also regulates control of each family's number of livestock, which consists of two milking cows and their offspring which have to be killed every three years. Islanders own two sheep per person; their offspring have to be killed on a yearly basis. A widow or widower is allowed only one cow. There's only one dog per family, but changes to this law need to be made to conform with new policies for keeping dogs! Ducks and chickens are mostly free range and kept by each family, on average about a dozen poultry per family. Dereck Rogers is Head of the Veterinary Department.

COMMUNICATIONS: responsible for Tristan Radio (the marine radio service based on the island); IT services and the internet café, headed by Andrea Repetto. The department also has responsibility for the island's local radio station, Atlantic FM and broadcaster, Laurian Rogers.

CONSERVATION: the Tristan Archipelago is regarded as the world's most important centre for the breeding of sea birds and two of the islands, Gough and Inaccessible, are UNESCO World Heritage Sites. More than 40% of the land is given over to nature conservation. Under its head, Trevor Glass (who has been specially trained in the UK, New Zealand and South Africa), the department works closely with the Royal Society for the Protection of Birds and the UK's Overseas Territories Environmental Programme to protect the island's wild creatures and plants and to curb the damage and destruction wrought by invasive species such as rats, house mice on Gough, loganberry at Sandy Point, the sagina plant on Gough, and New Zealand flax on Nightingale Island. They have vital responsibilities for the conservation of globally important species such as the Tristan albatross, the Atlantic yellow-nosed albatross, the sub-Antarctic fur seal and (unique to the Tristan archipelago) the Gough Bunting and the flightless bird known as the Inaccessible Rail. Their work is featured on the beautiful new definitive postage stamps issued by Tristan Post Office on 1 November 2010.

EDUCATION DEPARTMENT: responsible for the Education Service on Tristan including GCSEs. Jim Kerr is the Education Advisor; Head Teacher at St. Mary's School is Anne Green.

ISLAND STORE (the Tristan Supermarket, once known as the Canteen), responsible for retail supplies and all private orders of furniture, kitchenware, clothing and gas cylinders. It's part of Lorraine Repetto's remit at the Treasury.

MEDICAL DEPARTMENT: the Director of Medical Services is Dr Sridhar, whose responsibilities include the Camogli Hospital and dental care.

POLICE DEPARTMENT: responsible for Immigration and Customs (and thus the legal aspects of tourism and the status of incoming tourists); conservation inspection and laws (the implementation of legal measures to protect Tristan's unique biodiversity); search and rescue; 'everyday' policing and welfare (my job!).

POST OFFICE, Iris Green is head of what is more than just a postal service, as Tristan Post Office looks after the sales of the much-sought after stamps and coins for the island, preparing and despatching first day covers, special orders and mint and cancelled stamps to collectors all over the world – a vital part of the island's revenue.

PUBLIC WORKS DEPARTMENT (known to islanders as PWD), managed by expatriate Henning Myburgh, is responsible for masonry, carpentry, re-roofing and also, running the hardware store as well as electrical, plumbing and mechanical supplies and services.

TOURISM: coordinator and development officer, museum curator and handicraft store manager: Dawn Repetto.

TREASURY DEPARTMENT: responsible for banking, financing and accounts. Lorraine Repetto is in charge.

FISHING FACTORY: this is a private enterprise, currently run by the South African company Ovenstones Agencies (PTY) Ltd., responsible for processing and packing and freezing the local fishermen's catches of crayfish. The fishermen are employed by the company and go out fishing between 20 to 30 days a year to catch the set quota of 150 tons of crayfish for that year.

All islanders work a seven to eight hour day, from Monday to Friday. The school works a five-hour day. If there is a fishing day or offloading a cargo ship, then the working day will range from 10 to 15 hours, depending on the day's catch or weather.

Although Tristanians are living a very comfortable life on the island, this may not last. The average wage is £227 per month. People are given equal opportunity to apply for jobs and the retired workforce draws a small pension each week. The economy is on the decline. Expenditure continues to outweigh the revenue. If it keeps on like this, the island could be without money in two years or less (and this has been the major preoccupation of the Administrator who left in September 2010, David Morley). It's likely to be a priority for his replacement, Sean Burns, (formerly at the UK Embassy in Seoul, South Korea). It's the fishing that keeps our economy going at the moment. I hate to think what would happen to Tristan if the market for the fishing fell in value. Revenue from sales of Tristan stamps to collectors dropped away to virtually nothing for years because of internal problems, alienating loyal collectors. The lost revenue from the Post Office did not help our economic decline as it's the next most important source of revenue to our fishing industry. Our overall economic decline is the reason we had to bring in taxation. However, under the new Postmistress, Iris Green, the business has been revived to improved standards. There's an encouraging increase in this vital revenue and happy customers, who now enjoy good and attentive service. New attractive designs concentrate on island life and major British and royal anniversaries.

Now we have full British citizenship restored (it had been taken away under Mrs Thatcher), the younger people may like to make a life abroad. There are a few young people already carving a life for themselves in England. When they return, they bring new skills and fresh ideas to enrich our community.

If ever our economy fails, I can foresee the people leaving to look for better prospects abroad. Tristan could face an uncertain future with an ageing population. Many Tristanians will not agree with me, as they believe they will come through whatever fate has in store for Tristan. I can understand how they feel about this matter, and I hope and pray my fears never come to pass.

Even on Tristan, things move apace, and since *Rockhopper Copper* was first published in February 2005, Tristan and the community have seen quite a few changes: many of them have put the resolve of the Islanders' motto - 'Our Faith is our Strength' - to the test!

My family and I returned to Tristan in April 2005. I resumed my role as Inspector of Police, relieving Sgt. Dave Rogers, who returned to policing on St Helena.

2006 was a prosperous year for the Islanders. They had a very good fishing season. Eight cruise ships visited and over 1,000 passengers landed. Among the vessels was the RMS *St Helena*, which stayed for a week to celebrate the Tristan Quincentenary, the island of course, having been discovered by the Portuguese in 1506.

Many passengers from RMS *St Helena* stayed ashore with islanders during the week. Sales of *Rockhopper Copper* did really well, and the new venture on the sale of specially minted Tristan collectors' coins proved to be a good business investment by Mike Hentley, who was then Administrator.

To their astonishment, on Wednesday 7th June 2006, a group of islanders on a boat trip to Sandy Point found an oil rig grounded at Trypot Bay on the south side of Tristan. The rig was three stories high, about 100 metres by 100 metres square, and grounded about 200 metres from the shore. A few of the men scrambled on to the rig but found it deserted. On returning to the village, they reported what they had found.

The next day, amid driving rain and wind, I launched the police RIBs and led a party of islanders to carry out an official survey of the rig (Neil Swain, Mark Swain, Duncan Lavarello, Joe Green, Jack Green, Leon Glass, James Glass and Simon Glass, who was then Conservation Officer). Mark, Joe, Simon, James, and I carried out a thorough inspection, and found it deserted, but it had living accommodation, store-rooms, workshops, and four life boats.

We took photos and wrote what appeared to be the rig's registration number, which were sent to London by Anne Green, the Acting Administrator. We learned that the rig was named *A Turtle* and was owned by Catlera Oil Company, based in the Cayman Islands. It transpired that on 30th April 2006, the rig was being towed by the tug *Mighty Deliverer* from Brazil to Singapore, via Cape Town . The tug it seems, had been forced to release the rig during a storm: then it lost sight of it. The crew found it again 55 miles west of Tristan but lost it again in another storm. Despite help from another tug, *Ruby Deliverer,* the rig could not be located until it was found by the islanders.

After much correspondence between Tristan, London, and the owners, an attempt was made by the Dutch firm Smit Salvage, using the tug *St Zouros Hellas* to tow the rig away from Trypot Bay. The rescue mission to remove it was aborted, on 28th July 2006 after several weeks, because of the many setbacks and the bad weather.

The islanders were concerned that the rig would become a problem for the fishing grounds and penguin rookeries in the area. So on 29th December 2006, another attempt was made to remove it, this time by Titan Salvage supported by the tug *De Hong*, and the regular Tristan vessel, MFV *Kelso*. A few islanders were recruited to crew the RIBs ferrying men and equipment between the ship and the rig.

Finally, at 18.00 on 10th February 2007, the rig was towed ten miles from Tristan and sunk in 3,000 metres of water. Titan Salvage achieved this by cutting the top of the rig into small sections, mending its pontoon legs to give more buoyancy, thus towing away a much lighter rig. A full environmental survey and risk assessment had been carried out, so no damage was caused to the environment. A monitoring policy was drawn up to keep annual checks in the area - just in case the unforeseen happens.

Chris Bates (editor of *Rockhopper Copper*) visited Tristan with his wife Julie on board the SA *Agulhas* in September 2006. The three weeks Chris spent staying with me on Tristan, and his involvement in *Rockhopper Copper*, gave him an insight into island life. This led to him being appointed Tristan Government Representative in the UK, in which he has proved to be a great asset to the Tristan Government. This has enabled Tristan to have its point of view heard at conferences and events throughout the UK and as far as Réunion Island in the Indian Ocean, Ascension Island, the Cayman Islands, in the EU and with the European Commission.

In March 2007 I was elected as Chief Islander, along with a new Island Council. Little was I to know that the next three years would be momentous times, for me, the council and the community! I knew the Council and I had to address Tristan's serious economic situation (and this was before the global economic crisis hit all countries' economies). I informed the community of this during my speech at the first reception I hosted as Chief Islander.

Things grew worse on 13th February 2008. At 04.00 a devastating fire destroyed the fishing factory. The village had until recently only several hours' electricity supply each day, but then the factory stepped up its generation to supply 24-hour electricity. Now we only have one emergency generator to rely on.

The emergency work to repair the harbour, which was crumbling under the relentless swell of the South Atlantic, still went ahead. Without it, our community would have had no future. The cost was paid by the British Government's Department for International Development (DFID), with the work undertaken by the Ministry of Defence (MoD).

They gave the job the code name Operation Zest and sent a force of 40 sappers from 34 Field Squadron, 25 Engineer Regiment, Royal Engineers, supported by RFA *Lyme Bay* and ten medical staff from all three services under the command of Captain Paddy McAlpine RN as Joint Task Force Commander.

The RFA *Lyme Bay* arrived on 28th February and departed on 29th March 2008. During their time here, the members of the Task Force formed a close friendship with the community. This was highlighted when the ladies of the community cooked a traditional Tristan dinner for them: in true Tristan style, all island families participated. Captain Paddy said afterwards that the lads were eating cakes and pudding for a week – breakfast, lunch and dinner. Despite the long hours of hard work, all left Tristan having gained weight! It's true to say there was a feeling of emptiness felt throughout the community when the RFA *Lyme Bay* departed, such was the bond of friendship formed.

In 2010 this work on Tristan resulted in the British Army's top award for peace work, the Firmin Sword of Peace, being awarded to 34 Squadron Royal Engineers at their headquarters at Waterbeach in Cambridgeshire. It was presented by Brigadier Alastair Dickinson, Commander 8 Force Engineer Brigade.

Subsequently ferocious storms in June and August 2010 have badly damaged the harbour again and severely restricted its use. Emergency meetings have been held in London to consider the implications and to try to find a solution. Like most islanders, I believe the only long-term way forward is the construction of a new harbour: Pigbite is the site most frequently spoken of. The damage to the harbour is very, very serious: a 1,400 (metric) tonne concrete block at the end of the western breakwater has split, lifted and moved eastwards and one of the lifted parts is estimated to weigh 200 tonnes. The dolos* blocks, which are intended to dissipate the force of incoming waves to prevent damage to the harbour walls, were washed into the harbour entrance. The Tristan website (run jointly by the island government and the Tristan

[*A dolos is an unusually shaped, interlocking concrete block of about three tons, designed 50 years ago by South African Aubrey Kruger, to dissipate the force of the sea. Ten ton versions will be used for the repairs in 2011, costing £6 million]

da Cunha Association: www.tristandc.com) says this is a 'bitter blow' for Tristan and will force the island to seek help from DfID to enable essential repairs to be made. Without the Calshot harbour, fishing, freight and passenger traffic are all disrupted or impossible: it is the most basic lifeline for our community. Without it, could we sustain our community – or would we have to abandon our beloved island? The June storm, with swells of up to ten metres, had already damaged our fishing vessels and our cargo raft; fishing equipment and sea water pipes were damaged and blocks near the bait station end of the western breakwater were washed on to the quay – indeed, dolos blocks were deposited on it, such was the force of the storm.

With one problem solved (or so Tristanians thought early in 2008), another, potentially just as catastrophic, happened on the 11th April that year. Our large mobile crane broke beyond repair, thus restricting our ability to launch the fisheries patrol boat *Wave Dancer* and our large barge, *Atlantic Isle*. But help was at hand, with funding from the EU (EDF10) hopefully next year to continue work on the harbour, a modern gantry crane was installed. This made it possible to lift heavy equipment and the dolos, the interlocking concrete giant-jigsaw pieces which form the walls of the harbour

However, to further refurbish the harbour and carry out work around the factory in the area of the harbour shoreline, for which we wanted to use the South African contractors A.P.P.L.E Group, economically the Tristan Government was not in a good position. To help counter this, the Island council and I took a tough decision: to put austerity measures in place. After much deliberation and consultation with the community, the Council voted unanimously on 7th April 2008 to introduce an incremental taxation system that also ensures the lowest paid do not pay any tax on income.

Legislation to introduce income tax to Tristan for the first time came into effect from 1st June 2008. The tax rates set are for a person who earns:
- £1,500 per annum – pay no tax.
- £1,501- £3,000 per annum – 10%
- £3,001 upwards per annum – 13%
 (£ = one pound sterling, or GBP)

The community charge was increased from 1% to 3% and everyone is now required to contribute 4% for medical costs, except pensioners. This was brought in to enable the island to maintain its financial independence: the 21st century has finally caught up with Tristan!

In London, in the autumn of 2008, for the first time I attended the UK Overseas Territories Consultative Council, where prime ministers and leading representatives of these British territories discuss matters of mutual interest with British Government ministers, civil servants and specialists. There were also meetings with other Tristan 'stakeholders' - organisations and companies vital to our well being and prosperity. I was able to follow up on my report to London on the state of affairs on Tristan. So while there, I raised the profile of Tristan, letting those who govern Tristan from afar know how little help we had received from the UK and how isolated Tristan had been the past 17 years.

Now all has changed. There's a new mood of support, a new enthusiasm for us and genuine goodwill for our unique way of life from the officials with whom we deal. We've all got to know each other a great deal better. This friendly and positive spirit has led to an understanding of our wish to remain financially independent and to pay our way, while recognising that we will always need the support of outside bodies for capital projects beyond the financial scope of an island with fewer than 300 inhabitants. In my meetings with the then Minister for Overseas Territories, Gillian Merron and with many officials, I was able to emphasise that Tristan is most grateful for all the help and support provided by the UK Government. This positive attitude appears to have survived the changes in the UK's political landscape after its 2010 general election.

So, we have now had a Business Adviser, Julian Morris, visit and help Council put together a seven-year business plan for Tristan's future. We've had a Public Reform Sector Adviser, Stephen Catchpole, who drafted a reform plan to incorporate the business plan. Now on the island for two years (as at 2010), there's an expatriate manager for our Public Works Department, South African Henning Myburgh.

When the fishing factory was destroyed by fire, there was some concern on how the quota of crayfish should be caught at Tristan. To conserve the fishing grounds around Tristan and enable our islands to earn extra money, there was a policy agreement between the fishing concessionaires, Ovenstone Agencies (PTY) Ltd of South Africa and Tristan, that the quota of crayfish caught at Tristan would be done by Island fishermen, working from the island using small boats - not by the fishing ships using long lines, with traps attached. Tristan's fishing committee, James Glass (the Head of the Fisheries Department) and representatives from Ovenstones held a meeting to decide the most effective means to catch the fish. It was decided that the MFV *Kelso* would take on five small boats and ten island fishermen (two men per boat) to catch the quota. There being a total of 20 fishermen, each group would take a week, changing at each weekend. The crayfish caught were processed on board the MFV *Kelso* by her South African crew. It took from 22nd July 2008 to the middle of February 2009, to catch the quota. The majority of the fishermen experienced very rough weather, and could relate to what their fathers and grandfathers told them of the days they used to fish from the ships, using only small rowing boats. There were a few of the old fishermen who fished from the MFV *Kelso*, who used to fish in small 13 foot rowing dinghies. Now they have 27-foot boats powered by four cylinder diesel engines, with winches to haul the hoop-nets and traps.

Part of the extra help from the UK Government is an Education Advisor to improve standards of education and give in-service training to our teachers, as well as preparing for the raising of the school-leaving age to 16. He is our old friend Jim Kerr who, following his retirement as a head teacher in Hertfordshire, is back on the island with wife Sue, far from their home in Norfolk. Jim was the last expatriate teacher on Tristan and returned to the UK in February 1992. Both have settled into island life as if they haven't been away. At the time of writing, they'll be with us for another year.

To improve the quality of our infrastructure, a new post office, museum, craft shop, and police station have been built (with a grant from the UK's Foreign and Commonwealth Office) by A.P.P.L.E group. They will give a much better service to our island population, to our visitors, the customers around the world who collect our stamps - and the police station will meet the latest international human rights and legal obligations. And it'll be a much better place in which to work!

The new factory was completed for fishing trials on 1st July 2009 and it's now in operation. Very significantly, it is built to current EU standards and we are actively working to obtain accreditation from the European Commission for it and approval for our inspection regime, to enable us to sell our crayfish into the European Union countries – the largest single market in the world. Work is continuing on gaining this accreditation as I write this chapter. Discussions in Brussels with EC officials have proved very encouraging.

In September 2009 we had the significant news that changes in our status and relationship with St. Helena were to come into force. No longer would we (or Ascension Island) be a dependency of St. Helena. We would be on a more equal footing but the Governor for all three islands will remain based in Jamestown, St. Helena and we continue to benefit from some of St. Helena's resources, such as their Attorney General.

For me, there was one further and very significant surprise in store: the announcement that in the Queen's Birthdays Honours List for 2010, I had been awarded the MBE for services to the community of Tristan da Cunha. On the same day it was announced that, on behalf of the Governor of St. Helena, HM The Queen had awarded the Colonial Special Constabulary Medal to Lewis Glass and Lindsay Repetto and that Stanley Swain had been awarded the Colonial Fire Brigades Long Service Medal.

The most recent elections on the island (12th April 2010) saw Ian Lavarello voted in as Chief Islander, becoming the first member of the Lavarello family elected to the post.

Whatever the future holds for me, or wherever I may travel, I try to live by the code: I pass this way but once. Any good I can do, any kindness I show, let me do so now for I may not pass this way again. But wherever I may travel, a part of me will forever remain on Tristan.

APPENDIX

VISITING TRISTAN DA CUNHA

Tristan da Cunha is the most remote inhabited island in the world. It has no airport and only very limited access by sea and there are no hotels or restaurants. Visiting Tristan is not like making an excursion to Mablethorpe or a fortnight in Mallorca, agreeable though these are! However it is possible to make a visit and some planning (perhaps, indeed, a degree of ingenuity) is required. You can either visit as part of a cruise ship's itinerary or as an individual. If you wish to stay overnight, though, you will need to have the permission in advance of the Island Council and accommodation at a set rate (to include meals and laundry) will be arranged with a family or in a guest house. The number of berths on vessels serving the island restricts the number of people who can visit us and our journeys to the 'outside world' for medical treatment, study or holidays.

Firstly, it is suggested you look at the website operated jointly by the Tristan Government and the Tristan da Cunha Association (more about this organisation follows) on www.tristandc.com. This contains shipping schedules, current fares and any updates to conditions which may affect your application to stay on the island.

If you wish to visit as part of a cruise, then consider the voyages of Oceanwide Expeditions, a Dutch company operating the newly refurbished vessel MV *Plancius*. Their cruises are for about a hundred people with a serious interest in out-of-the-way places, the North and South Polar regions and remote islands. Their ships and crews are familiar with Tristan and have been able to help people visit Nightingale and Inaccessible Islands. In 2009, Sharon and I went to the 'Christening' of the *Plancius* in Vlissingen in The Netherlands. We were able to sample the comforts of the vessel overnight. Her voyages to Tristan are based on sailings from Europe, the Cape Verde Islands and South American ports. Website is www.oceanwide-expeditions; email: info@oceanwide-expeditions.com; Tel.+31 118 410 410.

They're not the only cruise operators calling at Tristan: it's worth therefore keeping in touch with a good travel agent specialising in individual travel or prepared to look out sailing of German and North American cruise lines who call at Tristan. Since the regular sailings of the RMS *St. Helena* were curtailed by the British Government, occasional voyages have been arranged. Be aware that every advertised sailing to the island fills up rapidly and that bad weather or heavy sea swells may curtail or make impossible landing on Tristan even when anchored off the island.

The other way is to plan to spend some time on the island and travel on one of the sailings of one of the ships serving the fish factory (which can carry up to 14 passengers, plus freight and mail). For this, you need to contact the Island Council through the Administration Office on Tristan (email: tristandcadmin@gmail.com) or phone +44 (0) 203 014 2001 (dialling code is the same as for the UK). Realistically, start to plan a couple of years before you intend to visit. All sailings are from Cape Town and you can ask us for advice and help in finding accommodation there. You'll need a valid passport and will have to pay a landing fee, the going rate for daily accommodation (which will be allocated to you) and you'll need good quality, waterproof, warm clothing and footwear to cope with our unpredictable and often wild climate. There is no bank on Tristan, so credit cards and debit cards are not accepted: bring either £ sterling, US $, Euro or South African rand or travellers' cheques in £ sterling.

Now if you're reading this with an eye to bringing a cruise ship or a party of special interest visitors (such as ornithologists, vulcanologists etc.), we will do our best to accommodate your wishes and the Tourism Development Officer, Dawn Repetto (who looks after our Museum and Handicraft Store) will be pleased to hear from you. You can contact her via email tourismtdc@gmail.com or by phone: +44 (0) 203 014 2037 - or get in touch with me via tristandcpolice@gmail.com or +44 (0) 203 014 2010.

There are restrictions on bringing in fresh fruit and vegetables, plants and seeds, as well as meat, fish and livestock – all designed to protect our unique and precious biodiversity. Import restrictions and duties on alcohol, tobacco and precious goods are similar to those in most 'Western' countries. Our increasing awareness of biodiversity security involves a special awareness of seeds and other unwelcome 'visitors' being unintentionally brought in on velcro strips, bootlaces and clothing and you may be asked to participate in thorough cleaning processes for them, either before boarding your ship or during the voyage. Invasive species have caused untold damage to the islands and our unique and precious wildlife and eradicating them now involves a vast amount of work and expenditure for our Conservation Department and their partners, such as the RSPB.

Moving to Tristan: It has been shown in the book that the island has again benefited from the experience and commitment of expatriates with specialist skills and knowledge and I hope they and their families will continue to be able to help us. It has been mooted in some quarters that we ought to consider inviting one or two families to move to the island on a longer-term basis – indeed, one English newspaper once interviewed me about the possibility of my job as island policeman being taken (when I stand down or retire) by an outsider. Nothing's impossible: but none of us should underestimate what might be involved for islanders and 'incomers'. If you're serious (and not just acting on some 'get-away-from-it-all' whim), get in touch and let's discuss the practicalities.

I have mentioned the Tristan da Cunha Association. This voluntary organisation publishes an excellent, full colour magazine twice a year containing news of the island and its people, as well as articles of historical and current interest on every aspect of Tristan. It organises an Annual Gathering (with a dinner dance and the possibility of an overnight stay in the hotel), usually in April in Southampton. The Association says of itself, quite simply, that it exists to serve the people of Tristan da Cunha and to foster good relations with them; also to promote interest in the Tristan Archipelago. In doing so, it hopes to encourage friendship among its members. The Association runs the Tristan Education Trust Fund which it hopes to use to develop education on the island

and always welcomes donations to this. Membership costs (at 2011 rates) £20 a year or £200 for life membership and an order form for membership (and the Association's publications) is on www.tristandc.com/assocorderform.php. Contributions to the Newsletter (and the website) should be sent to the Newsletter editor and Website Manager, Richard Grundy, at newseditor@tristandc.com or 'Solomon's', Queen Street, Keinton Mandeville, Somerset TA11 6EQ, UK.

*

Editor's Note: The UK Minister for the Overseas Territories, Henry Bellingham, announced in November 2010 that £6 million (GBP) would be spent by DfID on emergency repairs to the Tristan harbour, following 2010's storm damage. He said this should enable access to be maintained for passengers, medical evacuations, crayfish exports, freight and essential supplies. The crane which the contractors will use will be donated to the island.

GLOSSARY

You may find it helpful to have a glossary of some of the abbreviations I use in my work on Tristan da Cunha and in this book.

Berry fish	A pregnant crayfish which carries its egg sack under its tail.
Bushel	An imperial or US unit of dry volume, equivalent to 4 pecks or 8 gallons, used in agriculture for dry commodities.
Calshot	A coastal village in Hampshire, England, to which Tristanians were evacuated after the 1961 eruption, to live in former military married quarters until their return: www.southernlife.org.uk/calshot
Cambridge Expedition to Gough Island:	An expedition in 1955 to one of the last places on Earth of which little was known (part of the Tristan Archipelago): www.btinternet.com/.../gough_island/gough_island_expedition.html -
CID	Police Criminal Investigation Department
Clichés	Clusters of Penguin Chicks
Darwin Project	A UK Government funded conservation programme which has funded more than 700 projects including vital ones on Tristan: www.darwin.defra.gov.uk
DfID	The UK Government's Department for International Development: www.dfid.gov.uk
DEAT	South African Department of Environmental Affairs and Tourism: www.environment.gov.za

Denstone College	Co-educational boarding and day school in Staffordshire, England: www.denstonecollege.org
EC	European Commission – the executive body of the European Union: www.ec.europa.eu
EU	European Union: an economic and political union of 27 states, including the UK: www.europa.eu/abc/index_en.htm
Fatting Trip	A specific journey to Nightingale Island each year in longboats to hunt shearwaters (petrels) for their meat and fat. The fat was rendered into an oil used for cooking, roasting, frying etc.
Firmin	A company established in 1672, now based in Birmingham, UK, manufacturing and supplying requirements for state ceremonials, including swords and uniforms; sponsors of the British Army's highest award for peace work: www.firmin.co.uk
Five fingers	A striped fish caught around Tristan: delicious with chips!
HMS	Her (or His) Majesty's Ship
Interpol	International Criminal Police Organisation: www.interpol.int
Kitchener's Scouts	British military unit in the Second Boer War, correctly Kitchener's Fighting Scouts: www.angloboerwar.com
Lake District	A national park in North West England: www.lakedistrict.gov.uk
Longboat	A traditional open boat powered by oars or sail used on Tristan.
Mablethorpe	Traditional English seaside resort on the Lincolnshire coast, first praised by Tennyson: www.mablethorpeholidays.com
Mallorca	Balearic Island especially popular with North Europeans for holidays: www.mallorcaonline.com

MBE	The Most Excellent Order of the British Empire, an order of chivalry established on 4 June 1917, comprising five classes in civil and military divisions, including Member of the Order of the British Empire.
MFV	Motor Fishing Vessel
MS	Motor Ship
MV	Motor Vessel
The Patches	Allotments of various sizes, enclosed by dry-stone walls. Located three and a half miles west of Edinburgh-of-the-Seven-Seas, used by islanders to grow potatoes and vegetables. Weekend cottages are situated here and the area is the terminus of the world's most remote regularly-timetabled bus service.
Percy Fitzpatrick Institute:	The Percy FitzPatrick Institute of African Ornithology (affectionately known as the Fitztitute) at the University of Cape Town: www.fitzpatrick.uct.ac.za
PVC	A plastic-based material for fittings used in buildings etc.
PWD	Public Works Department of Tristan da Cunha
RAF	(United Kingdom) Royal Air Force: www.raf.mod.uk
RFA	Royal Fleet Auxiliary
RIB	Rigid Inflatable Boat
RMS	Royal Mail Ship: (sometimes used by islanders as an abbreviation for the RMS *St. Helena*).
RSJ	A steel girder used in buildings
RSPB	A UK-based charity (supported by more than a million members) 'working to secure a healthy environment for birds and all wildlife': www.rspb.org.uk

163

SA	South Africa or South African Ship
SAAF	South African Air Force: www.af.mil.za
SAS	South African Naval Ship
SS	Steam Ship
Tristan da Cunha Association	An organisation for people linked to or interested in Tristan: www.tristandc.com
Tristan Times	On line island newspaper: www.tristantimes.com
VHF	Very High Frequency (FM)
WPC	Woman Police Constable
Zodiacs	A brand name for a type of inflatable pontoon made of rubber.